Learning to
THEORIZE

Learning to
THEORIZE

A Four-Step Strategy

Dennis E. Mithaug

Sage Publications, Inc.
International Educational and Professional Publisher
Thousand Oaks ▪ London ▪ New Delhi

For information:

 Sage Publications, Inc.
2455 Teller Road
Thousand Oaks, California 91320
E-mail: order@sagepub.com

Sage Publications Ltd.
6 Bonhill Street
London EC2A 4PU
United Kingdom

Sage Publications India Pvt. Ltd.
M-32 Market
Greater Kailash I
New Delhi 110 048 India

Printed in the United States of America

Library of Congress Cataloging-in-Publication Data

Mithaug, Dennis E.
  Learning to theorize: A four-step strategy / by Dennis E. Mithaug
    p.   cm.
  Includes bibliographical references and index.
  ISBN 0-7619-0979-6 (cloth: alk. paper)
  ISBN 0-7619-0980-X (pbk.: alk. paper)
    1. Social sciences—Philosophy.   I. Title.
  H61 .M543 2000
  300—dc21   00-008362

This book is printed on acid-free paper.

00   01   02   03   04   05   06   7   6   5   4   3   2   1

Acquiring Editor:	C. Deborah Laughton
Editorial Assistant:	Eileen Carr
Production Editor:	Diane S. Foster
Editorial Assistant:	Victoria Cheng
Typesetter/Designer:	Lynn Miyata
Cover Designer:	Michelle Lee

For Cathy

Contents

Preface

To theorize is to engage in the art of explanation. People who master the art know how to collect ideas, analyze content, and marshal conclusions in the most cogent reasoning possible. They can construct new understanding from old uncertainty by identifying what is credible but not valuable and what is valuable but not credible. That allows them to transform their tentative ideas into robust explanations that render the unusual usual and the confusing clear.

The four-step thinking strategy described in this book will help you become a master of explanation. You can use the strategy to address the technical questions and issues of your profession or to deal with the practical confusions of everyday life. Constructive theorizing is universal in its application to those thinking and reasoning problems that challenge your understanding of how things work, how they ought to work, and what should be done about them. You can use the strategy anytime, anywhere.

I wrote this book to help students in education and the social sciences improve their beliefs about important empirical, moral, and policy issues. I call the strategy constructive theorizing because it guides the *construction* of explanations for uncertainties that students want to understand and because it results in a *theory* that reduces discrepancies between their beliefs and uncertainties. Students in psychology, sociology, political science, and education benefit from the approach because it complements their training in research, policy, and professional practice. For example, theorizing about how the individual and society function, which is a focus in psychology and sociology, is complemented by the strategy's approach to understanding the moral and political implications of explanations of fact. And theorizing about policy and practice, which is a focus in political science and education, is complemented by the strategy's approach to understanding the empirical and moral basis for prescriptions to act.

Constructive theorizing will help you understand how claims for social action depend upon the credibility and worth of theories of fact and value and how claims about how things work affect the credibility and worth of theories of judgment and action. The strategy untangles these interdependent issues in a way recommended by Edwards and Lippucci in their book *Practicing American Politics* (1998). These authors also believe that students should learn to distinguish between fact, judgment, and action:

> Although these three questions—what is, what's right, and what works—are often intertwined in any dispute, asking them separately helps students to pinpoint areas of consensus and disagreement. In the case of welfare policy, for example, they will discover that some people agree that a welfare problem exists (what is) and may even agree on what's right (that certain people should or should not receive a helping hand from the rest of society), but they may not agree on what works (what welfare reforms would best address the problem). (Edwards & Lippucci, 1998, p. xxv)

Simply stated, constructive theorizing is problem solving to understand why a circumstance is inconsistent with a belief about how things work, how to judge them, and what to do about them. In the book, you will use it to construct empirical theories to explain a circumstance, moral theories to judge the significance of that condition, and policy theories to prescribe actions to alter or maintain it. In the process, you will learn to ask questions and find answers that lead to your own explanations for circumstances you do not understand.

The first step of the four-step strategy defines problems of not understanding as discrepancies between what you know and what you don't know about the event or situation. This focuses your attention on the missing information that may explain the inconsistency. The second step is a search for information and a constructed explanation that changes the condition of not knowing into a condition of knowing. The third step evaluates the credibility and worth of the explanation constructed in Step 2. Credibility assessments determine the coherence, validity, and verifiability of the explanation, and value assessments determine the significance, scope, and utility of the new theory. The fourth step adjusts existing beliefs about the circumstance by repeating the four-step strategy to eliminate other inconsistencies between the new theory and existing beliefs.

This strategy for learning to theorize is similar to other widely adopted self-discovery strategies. One is the scientific method introduced in the 17th century by Isaac Newton (Hellemans & Bunch, 1988). That approach also includes steps that define unknowns, collect information, construct hypotheses (theories), and test predictions (Random House, 1995, p. 1201). A second is the method of practical reasoning described in the pioneering research of Newell and Simon (1972), who identified the three-step strategy that humans use to solve complex problems (pp. 661-784). The third is the self-regulated learning approach of getting learners to define problems that will provoke them into learning on their own. All three approaches are consistent with the four-step theorizing strategy of this book.

THE APPROACH

Viewing constructive theorizing as a first cousin to problem solving, practical reasoning, and self-regulated learning suggests what is unique to the strategy. It is a method of learning to theorize about *one class of problems*: questions about how things work, how they ought to work, and what to do about them. It is a type of *practical reasoning* that promises to improve adjustments to the unusual circumstances provoking these questions. It is a type of *self-regulated learning* to explain circumstances *you do not understand*. Finally, the method is a form of *tentative knowing* in that the credibility and worth of a theory constructed by the method are always contingent upon future events being consistent with its explanation.

Chapter 1 compares everyday problem solving with the scientific problem solving of people like Johann Kepler, Charles Darwin, and Albert Einstein. It shows how both types of problem solving are provoked by inconsistencies between circumstances and beliefs. The chapter also compares the scientific method with problem-solving paradigms in the social sciences and education to show that the structure and format they share are similar to those of constructive theorizing. This leads to a discussion of how constructive theorizing builds upon these strategies by requiring you to engage in inductive and deductive reasoning to construct new explanations for how things work, how they ought to work, and what to do about them.

The chapter concludes by using this four-step strategy to explain the unusual circumstances that led Casey Martin, a golfer with a disability, to gain permission from the Professional Golf Association (PGA) to use a cart during tournament play. This event was unusual because there seemed to be no reason for Casey Martin to request a cart (empirical question). There was no basis for judging whether it was right for him to make the request (moral question). And there was no precedent for the PGA to honor or reject it (policy question).

Chapter 2 describes how constructive theorizing functions like practical reasoning to explain changing circumstances. The chapter argues that because beliefs guide expectations, choices, and actions, they set in motion an adjustment process that uses experience with the past to predict circumstances in the future. In this context, constructive theorizing is a strategy for constructing explanations that are consistent with the circumstances affecting our adjustments (they are credible) and that are helpful in guiding our actions to improve those adjustments (they are valuable). The chapter explains why holding beliefs supported by credible and valuable theories is better in a practical sense than holding beliefs that are not supported by credible and valuable theories.

It also explains why the standards of coherence, validity, and verifiability are appropriate for evaluating the credibility of a theory's explanations for unknown circumstances and why the standards of significance, scope, and utility are appropriate to evaluate a theory's value in adjusting to those circumstances. By using these criteria to decide which theories to keep and which to reject, you will discover how well your circumstances are governed by your beliefs.

Chapters 3 through 5 show how the use of constructive theorizing will help you analyze and understand complex social issues of not knowing what to believe—issues that are connected in a web of ideological thinking that claims to be the only way of knowing what to believe. The chapters show how you can improve your beliefs about why some people experience unusually difficult circumstances and, as a consequence, persistently fail to get what they need and want in life. This more challenging use of constructive theorizing illustrates its recursive nature: that theories constructed to explain one complex situation often provoke new inconsistencies with other theories, thereby necessitating more theorizing to resolve those contradictions.

For example, in Chapter 3 on empirical theorizing, resolving inconsistencies between competing explanations about how things work provokes new questions about how things should work for people in need. Then, in Chapter 4, moral theorizing to answer this question provokes new questions about what should be done, if anything. Finally, in Chapter 5, policy theorizing to resolve these inconsistencies provokes new questions again about what works. Figure P.1 illustrates this cyclical pattern of theorizing to resolve inconsistencies among interdependent beliefs about how things work, how they ought to work, and what should be done about them.

LIMITATIONS

Although I believe this method will help you learn to theorize, it is by no means the only way to learn. You can learn to theorize effectively without any strategy at all. So the method is not necessary to become effective at the art. Even Newton, who claimed to use a version of the scientific method to formulate his theories of motion, probably did not follow it in a lockstep manner, as Hellemans and Bunch (1988) pointed out:

> Newton called his method the "method of analysis and synthesis," a procedure that included both an inductive and deductive stage. Theories are formulated from observations; these theories are then used to predict other phenomena. However, in practice, science does not operate strictly according to scientific method. Newton's most important discoveries were probably the product of intuition, which he later backed up with experiment, reasoning, and mathematics. (Hellemans & Bunch, 1988, pp. 146-147)

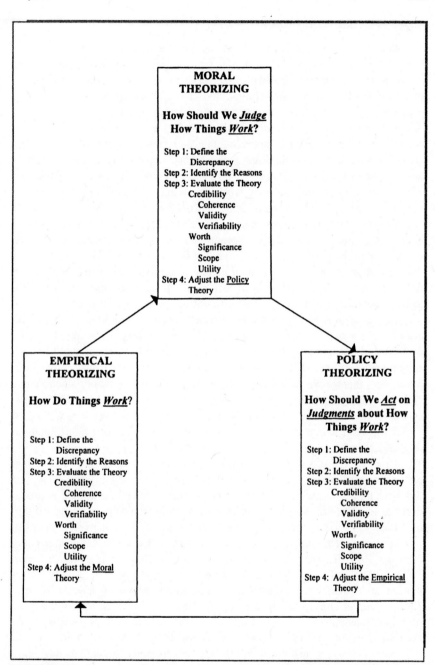

FIGURE P.1. Recursive Theorizing to Solve an Empirical, Moral, and Policy Problem

A second limitation of the method is that it does not offer any enduring knowledge about what is true and good about our material and social world. It is of no use, for example, when identifying, constructing, or evaluating the credibility or worth of metaphysical truths, self-evident truths, or truths based upon human nature or natural law. The method can only help you find solutions to problems created by circumstances that you experience, observe, or can act upon in some manner. Therefore, any theory produced by the method is temporary because it is *instrumental* to understanding these relationships. Moreover, any change in circumstances can affect a new theory's credibility and value, just as any change in the theorizer's needs and goals can produce new perspectives on what constitutes an inconsistency worth resolving. Either change can create a need to understand and a corresponding provocation to theorize.

Viewing theories as instruments for understanding suggests a third question about the strategy's limitations. Because constructive theorizers are free to choose the problems they want to solve, the information they deem relevant to those solutions, and the arrangement of that information to form explanations, won't the result reflect their unique needs, interests, and capacities? And won't it misrepresent the "true nature" of the circumstances being explained?

This is a question that can be directed toward all modes of theorizing because every one of these strategies involves individuals' defining their own problems of not knowing something. Hence, any resulting claim about knowledge must be supported by a test for its credibility and worth. Constructive theorizing does this by evaluating credibility with checks on the theory's coherence, validity, and verifiability and by evaluating worth with checks on its significance, scope, and utility. The expectation is that independent thinkers will adopt a new theory if it is true and valuable enough to improve their adjustments in thinking and acting.

This discussion suggests yet another limitation. Because the book offers only conceptual guidance on how to evaluate a theory's credibility and value, you will have to look elsewhere to get more detailed direction on the particular procedures to employ. For more information on evaluating the coherence and validity of a theory, I recommend Alec Fisher's *The Logic of Real Arguments* (1988), Antony Flew's *Thinking Straight* (1977), David Kelley's *The Art of Reasoning* (1994), C. A. Missimer's *Good Arguments* (1995), Douglas Walton's *Informal Logic* (1989), and John Wilson's *Thinking With Concepts* (1995). And for information on a theory's verifiability, I recommend Huey-tsyh Chen's *Theory-Driven Evaluations* (1990) because it provides an excellent analysis of the types of evaluations appropriate for empirical and normative (policy) theories. C. E. Harris's *Applying Moral Theories* (1992) and Hugh Mercer Curtler's *Ethical Argument* (1993) are also useful in learning how to verify moral theories.

Procedural tests for significance, scope, and utility are the least well developed and as a result have fewer supporting references. Again, *Theory-Driven*

Evaluations (Chen, 1990) may be useful. It describes three criteria that policy makers can use in selecting empirical studies for their policy arguments:

> *relevance* (how closely and clearly did the content of the study relate to the administrator's area of responsibility?); the *trust test* ([do] . . . the results match up with previous experience, knowledge, and values?); and the *utility test* ([does] . . . the research show how to make plausible changes in things that can plausibly be changed? Does the research challenge any current philosophy, program, or practice? Does it offer new perspectives or does it support the status quo?) (p. 69)

Another resource is David Fetterman's (1996) empowerment evaluation, which defines worth criteria in terms of the circumstances being judged (pp. 5-6).

Chapter 6 places some of these limitations in context by reminding you that constructive theorizing is only a guide to getting answers to questions of not knowing something. Its purpose is to help you think clearly about confusing and ill-defined circumstances so you can construct your own theories and hypotheses about those conditions. The strategy enables those who initially have no idea what to propose by way of a theory or explanation to come up with full-blown theories and hypotheses that can direct their inquiries. In *Proposals That Work,* Locke, Spirduso, and Silverman (1993) argued that achieving this result is necessary early in any proposal to study important phenomena:

> *All research emerges from a perceived problem,* some unsatisfactory situation in the world that we want to confront. Sometimes the difficulty rests simply in the fact that we don't understand *how things work* and have the human itch to know. At other times we are confronted by decisions [about *how to judge things*] or the *need for action* when the alternatives or consequences are unclear. Such perceived problems are experienced as a disequilibrium, a dissonance in our cognition. Notice, however, they do not exist out in the world, but in our minds.
>
> That may sound at first like one of those "nice points" of which academics are sometimes fond, but for the purposes of a novice researcher, locating the problem in the right place and setting up your understanding of exactly what is unsatisfactory may represent much more than an arbitrary exercise. *Thinking clearly about problems, questions, hypotheses, and research purposes can prevent mental log jams that sometimes block or delay clear identification of what is to be investigated* [italics added]. (p. 46)

This chapter also gives you three sample topics on which you can practice your own brand of constructive theorizing. The first is elite athletes with disabilities, the second is the accelerating universe, and the third is cloning. The three topics raise interesting empirical, moral, and policy questions. The chapter includes a constructive theorizing checklist in the use of the strategy along with a list of *New York Times* articles on the three topics to stimulate your inquiry. It also provides a summary of the claims, terms, and processes of constructive theorizing and a list of the theories constructed in the book. Hopefully, this will get you started theorizing on your own.

Knowing What to Believe

This book introduces a method of theorizing that is similar to everyday problem solving and practical reasoning. It is a version of self-regulated learning to improve your own explanations for how things work, how they ought to work, and what should be done to improve them. To illustrate, consider John Dewey's (1933) lost traveler, who exhibited some of the same problem solving and practical reasoning you might engage in if you were in his shoes. This traveler came to a fork in road and did not know which route to take. This situation was unsettling in that it featured a discrepancy between what he wanted to know—how to get to his destination—and the information his circumstances provided—two possible paths to take. Therefore, the traveler was motivated to solve the problem of not knowing which path to choose. He searched his memory for possible clues and then searched the surrounding area by climbing trees to find evidence in support of one belief or the other about which path was right.

JOHN DEWEY'S LOST TRAVELER

A man traveling in an unfamiliar region comes to a branching of the road. Having no sure knowledge to fall back upon, he is brought to a standstill of hesitation and suspense. Which road is right? And how shall his perplexity be resolved? There are but two alternatives: he must either blindly and arbitrarily take his course, trusting to luck for the outcome, or he must discover grounds for the conclusion that a given road is right. Any attempt to decide the matter by thinking will involve inquiring into other facts, whether brought to mind by memory, or by further observation, or by both. The perplexed wayfarer must carefully scrutinize what is before him and he must cudgel his memory. He looks for evidence that will support belief in favor of either of the roads—for evidence that will weigh down one suggestion. He may climb a tree; he may go first in this direction, then in that, looking, in either case, for signs, clues, indications. He wants something in the nature of signboard or a map, and his reflection is aimed at the discovery of facts that will serve this purpose. (Dewey, 1933, p. 14)

Solving practical problems like this is similar to constructive theorizing in that it is motivated by a discrepancy between a circumstance and an expectation—a fork in the road with no sign indicating where the roads lead and the expectation that only one road is the right one. Practical problem solving, like constructive theorizing, resolves inconsistencies. When we do it, we *search for facts* that suggest one road rather than the other, and then we *test our hypothesis* by taking the path we believe is the right one. If the road suggested by our hypothesis is confirmed, we conclude that our belief about it is credible and valuable. It is credible because it is consistent with the facts (the road leads where we expect), and it is valuable because acting on that belief (about where the road leads) gets us where we want to go. Last, we *adjust our beliefs* about the fork in the road by keeping the hypothesis that turned out to be credible and valuable and rejecting the one that was neither credible nor valuable.

The four steps of constructive theorizing are similar. They are (a) defining the discrepancy between an existing belief and a circumstance, (b) finding reasons to explain the discrepancy, (c) evaluating the credibility and worth of the reasons and explanation, and (d) adjusting existing beliefs so that they are consistent with the new explanation.

There are also some differences between the two approaches. One is that constructive theorizing always solves problems of not knowing something. Consequently, its first step defines problems of not knowing what to believe as *discrepancies* between knowing and not knowing the *facts,* the *values* attached to those facts, or the *actions* justified by those facts and values. This classifies discrepancy problems as (a) problems of not knowing *how things work,* which are *empirical problems* of not knowing the cause of a circumstance (the facts); (b) problems of not knowing *how to judge* a circumstance, which are *moral problems* of not knowing what standard to use to judge a circumstance (the values attached to the facts); and (c) problems of not knowing *how to act,* which are *policy problems* of not knowing what collective action to take (the actions based on facts and values).

A second difference is the result of this search *for reasons to explain* discrepancies. It is not a problem solved but rather a theory constructed. Consequently, when the search is for *facts* to explain the circumstance that we do not understand, the result is an empirical theory. When the search is for *values* to judge the explanation of that circumstance, the result is a moral theory. And when the search is for prescriptions for *actions* that are consistent with that explanation and judgment, the result or solution is a policy theory.

A third difference is the method's evaluation of results. It uses standards somewhat different from those determining the effectiveness of solutions to various problems. This is necessary because the method produces a theory purporting to be knowledge about something. Hence, it is important that the knowledge be credible in the sense of being coherent, valid, and true. It is also important that it be valuable in the sense of being significant, comprehensive, and useful. Knowledge that meets these criteria helps us decide what to believe about how things work, how they ought to work, or what we should do about them.

The last difference is that this method of thinking always produces temporary solutions, whereas general problem solving often produces permanent solutions. This characteristic is reflected in the fourth step of the method, which checks for inconsistencies between the new theory and other theories and beliefs and then resolves them with additional theorizing.

This chapter describes some of these characteristics. The next section illustrates how constructive theorizing is similar to problem solving, practical reasoning, and self-regulated learning. Each comparison ends with a table showing the correspondence between the steps typically used in these processes and the steps of constructive theorizing. The last section demonstrates differences between constructive theorizing and these other strategies by using it to solve a contemporary problem of not knowing something—why Casey Martin, a golfer with a physical disability, requested to use a golf cart during tournament play. This shows how explaining unusual circumstances in life is different from discovering the correct path to town.

THEORIZING AND A COMMON PROCESS

Comparing constructive theorizing with the reasoning of Dewey's lost traveler shows it to be a derivative of a common process, a pattern of thinking that all of us engage in whether we recognize it as theorizing or not. The following discussion compares constructive theorizing with scientific problem solving, practical reasoning, and the self-regulated learning that all independent thinkers engage in to find answers to questions about an unknown or disturbing event.

Theorizing as Problem Solving

Constructive theorizing is similar to practical problem solving in two ways. First, both strategies commence with a discrepancy condition. Second, both methods are based on the four steps of the scientific method. Let us examine the first similarity by reviewing the scientific problem solving of world-class theorizers like Johann Kepler, Charles Darwin, and Albert Einstein. This will reveal how they too were provoked into theorizing by an inconsistency very similar to the one that prompted Dewey's lost traveler to search for the right road. Consider, for example, the inconsistency that led Kepler to develop a new theory of orbiting planets. He noticed with some surprise and distress that Brahe's measurements of the positions of stars and planets showed Mars to be off by as much as 8 minutes of arc from the position predicted by Ptolemaic theory of circular motion. This was troubling because there was no reasonable explanation for the inconsistency. Kepler could not accept the possibility that God's universe was mathematically inconsistent, nor did he believe that Brahe's measurements were inaccurate. This left the possibility that Ptolemaic theory was inaccurate and that the planets did not revolve in circular orbits. Kepler resolved this inconsistency by constructing a theory of elliptical orbits, which he could verify mathematically. His new theory forever changed our understanding of orbiting planets.

Now let us consider what motivated Charles Darwin to develop a new theory of evolution. For starters, Darwin, like many of his contemporaries, believed that all organisms were created perfectly by God. The problem with this belief was that Darwin also believed the geologic evidence indicating that environments change over time. This troubled him. The following passage by Howard E. Gruber (1974) explains why:

> He [Darwin] began with a notion of a stable, harmonious natural order, in which all organic beings were adapted to each other and to their physical environment in a fashion ordained by the Creator. As he came to accept modern geological views of a constantly changing order in the physical world, *a contradiction within his point of view developed* as follows: each species was adapted to its milieu; the milieu was undergoing constant change; and yet the species were changeless. Darwin probably began *to feel this contradiction* during the final months of the voyage, as he was going over his notes and organizing his materials [italics added]. It was not until July 1837, ten months after returning to England, that he began his first notebook on "Transmutation of Species." It was over a year after that, in September 1838, that the role of natural selection in evolution began to be clear to him. (p. 20)

Albert Einstein was also troubled by inconsistencies between circumstances and beliefs. The one that got him started theorizing about relativity was that the theory of magnetism could explain why current flows through a wire when a magnet rotates around the wire but *could not explain* why current also flows through the wire when the wire rotates around the magnet. This made no sense to him. So he constructed a theory that was consistent with these facts. Unfortunately, his new view—the theory of relativity—created another inconsistency with an existing belief: that the velocity of light was variable. Einstein resolved this by claiming that the speed of light was constant and then plugging that value into his theory to prove the theory and the claim. Morris (1983) explained Einstein's motivation to theorize as follows:

> The Einsteinian universe was a strange one. At least it appeared strange to physicists accustomed to the "commonsense" views that were embodied in the nineteenth-century physics. . . . Physicists who studied his theories in detail

soon recognized that Einstein had introduced his new ideas about the nature of time and space not because he was in love with the bizarre, but because he wanted to weld physics into a harmonious whole. He had propounded this theories of relativity *because he had felt that the old physics was not as logical or consistent as it should be* [italics added]. (p. 28)

The second way that constructive theorizing is similar to problem solving is through its correspondence with the four steps of the scientific method: (a) Identify a problem, (b) collect relevant data on the problem, (c) formulate a hypothesis to explain the problem, and (d) test the hypothesis (Random House, 1995, p. 1201). That method dates back to the 19th century and has had a paradigmatic influence throughout the sciences since. You can see its imprint in research proposals and dissertations (Lock et al., 1993, p. 168), journal articles (American Psychological Association, 1993, pp. 22-27), in the junior high school social studies curriculum (Lewis, 1991, 1998), and in popular magazine articles on problem solving (for a discussion of several examples, see Stone, 1988, p. 7). Deborah Stone's (1988) policy sciences approach to problem solving illustrates one of its adaptations: (a) Identify objectives to solve a problem or meet a need, (b) identify alternative courses of action for achieving objectives, (c) predict and evaluate the possible consequences of each alternative, and (d) select the alternative that maximizes the attainment of objectives (p. 5). There are many other applications, some deviating creatively from the standard four steps. Consider the examples below.

In *Public Policy in the Eighties,* Bullock, Anderson, and Brady (1983) identified a five-stage approach to policy: (a) problem definition, (b) policy agenda (deciding which problems to address), (c) policy formulation and adoption (considering options and selecting the best alternative), (d) policy implementation (implementing the solution), and (e) policy evaluation (evaluating the effects of the solution and recommending adjustments) (pp. 6-9). In *Policy Analysis for the Real World,* Hogwood and Gunn (1984) expanded the paradigm to nine steps: defining the problem by deciding to decide, deciding how to decide, and issue forecasting; considering alternatives by setting objectives and priorities through policy implementation, monitoring, and control; and evaluating and reviewing during policy maintenance, succession, or termination. In *Policy Analysis by Design,* Bobrow and Dryzek (1987) identified five steps: (a) Interpret the problem and performance goals (definition of the problem); (b) identify and collect needed information (more problem definition); (c) invent and stipulate policy alternatives (consideration of alternatives); (d) assess and compare policy alternatives (implementation and evaluation of solutions); and (e) construct arguments (adjustment of the process) (pp. 208-211).

The problem-solving paradigms used by decision makers in business and industry are similar. In *Decision Making: A Psychological Analysis of Conflict,*

Choice, and Commitment, Janis and Mann (1977) identified seven steps for high-quality decision making: (a) Thoroughly canvas a wide range of alternative courses of action; (b) survey the full range of objectives to be fulfilled and values implicated by the choice; (c) carefully weight the positive and negative consequences of each alternative; (d) intensively search for new information and evaluate alternatives; (e) correctly assimilate new information; (f) reexamine positive and negative consequences of alternatives; and (g) detail provisions for implementing chosen alternatives (p. 11). Robin Hogarth (1980) recommended a similar sequence in *Judgement and Choice: The Psychology of Decision*: (a) Structure the problem, (b) assess consequences, (c) assess uncertainties, (d) evaluate alternatives, (e) analyze sensitively, (f) gather information, and (g) choose (p. 130).

Less creative variations of the problem-solving paradigm abound in psychology and education. D'Zurilla and Golfried (1971), for example, identified four steps to modifying the behavior of individuals: (a) problem definition and formulation, (b) generation of alternatives, (c) decision making, and (d) verification. Whitman, Burgio, and Johnston (1984) identified five steps to conduct cognitive-behavioral interventions: (a) thinking of life as an ongoing process of solving problems, (b) defining completely and operationally the problem situation, (c) generating a list of possible solutions, (d) deciding on a particular solution, and (e) implementing the solution and matching outcomes with expectations. Haaga and Davison (1986) also recommended a five-step strategy when proving therapy for individuals: (a) problem orientation, (b) problem definition and formulation, (c) generation of alternatives, (d) decision making, and (e) solution implementation and verification. And Rose (1982) recommended a four-step approach for group therapy: (a) Analyze the problem, (b) discover new approaches to solving it, (c) evaluate approaches, and (d) develop strategies for implementing approaches in real world.

The point of this list is perhaps obvious. There is little that is new about the structure of constructive theorizing. It follows the same logic as the scientific method and its many derivatives. Table 1.1 compares the steps of the three versions: scientific problem solving, general problem solving, and four-step constructive theorizing. See if you can detect their relationship to John Dewey's original formulation of the problem-solving strategy: "What is the problem?" "What are the alternatives?" and "Which alternative is best?" (quoted in Simon, 1960, p. 3).

Theorizing as Practical Reasoning

Constructive theorizing is also a type of practical reasoning that moves thinkers from a condition of not knowing to a condition of knowing. John Dewey's analysis of practical reasoning in *How We Think* (1910/1991) and

TABLE 1.1

Comparing Scientific Problem Solving and General Problem Solving With Constructive Theorizing

Scientific Problem Solving	*General Problem Solving*	*Constructive Theorizing*
1. Identify a problem as an inconsistency between facts of a circumstance and existing theory.	1. Define the problem.	1. Define the discrepancy problem of not knowing, and collect relevant data describing the difference between knowing and not knowing something.
2. Collect relevant data on the problem.	2. Find a method to solve it.	2. Find reasons and construct a theory to explain it.
3. Formulate a hypothesis to explain the problem.	3. Implement the method.	3. Evaluate the credibility and worth of the theory.
4. Test the hypothesis.	4. Evaluate the solution.	4. Adjust beliefs inconsistent with the theory by repeating Steps 1 through 3.

Newell and Simon's research on means-ends reasoning in *Human Problem Solving* (1972) reflect these parallels.

Dewey's (1910/1991) practical reasoning comes in "five logically distinct steps: (i) a felt difficulty; (ii) its location and definition; (iii) suggestion of possible solution; (iv) development of reasoning on the bearings of the suggestion; (v) further observation and experiment leading to its acceptance or rejection; that is, the conclusion of belief or disbelief" (p. 72). Dewey illustrated his method with three problems, which move a thinker from not knowing to (a) knowing how to get to a meeting, (b) knowing the function of a white pole on a boat, and (c) knowing the origin of bubbles appearing on a drinking glass. He stated that

> the first [problem] illustrates the kind of thinking done by every one during a day's business, in which neither the data, nor the ways of dealing with them, take one outside the limits of everyday experience. . . . The second case forms a natural transition; its materials lie well within the bounds of everyday, unspecialized experience; but the problem, instead of being directly involved in the person's businesses, arises indirectly out of his activity. . . . [And the third is] a

case in which neither problem nor mode of solutions would have been likely to occur except to one with some prior *scientific training* [italics added]. (p. 71)

The problems are presented as follows:

1. The other day when I was downtown on 16th Street a clock caught my eye. I saw that the hands pointed to 12.20. This suggested that I had an engagement at 124th Street, at one o'clock. I reasoned that as it had taken me an hour to come down on a surface car, I should probably be twenty minutes late if I returned the same way. I might save twenty minutes by a subway express. But was there a station near? If not, I might lose more than twenty minutes in looking for one. Then I thought of the elevated, and I saw there was such a line within two blocks. But where was the station? If it were several blocks above or below the street I was on, I should lose time instead of gaining it. My mind went back to the subway express as quicker than the elevated; furthermore, I remembered that it went nearer than the elevated to the part of 124th Street I wished to reach, so that time would be saved at the end of the journey. I concluded in favor of the subway, and reached my destination by one o'clock.

2. Projecting nearly horizontally from the upper deck of the ferryboat on which I daily cross the river, is a long white pole, bearing a gilded ball at its tip. It suggested a flagpole when I first saw it; its color, shape, and gilded ball agreed with this idea, and these reasons seemed to justify me in this belief. But soon difficulties presented themselves. The pole was nearly horizontal, an usual position for a flagpole; in the next place, there was no pulley, ring, or cord by which to attach a flag; finally, there were elsewhere two vertical staffs from which flags were occasionally flown. It seemed probable that the pole was not there for flag-flying.

I then tried to imagine all possible purposes of such a pole, and to consider for which of these it was best suited: *(a)* Possibly it was an ornament. But as all the ferryboats and even the tugboats carried like poles, this hypothesis was rejected. *(b)* Possibly it was the terminal of a wireless telegraph. But the same considerations made this improbable. Besides, the more natural place for such a terminal would be the highest part of the bow, on top of the pilot house. *(c)* Its purpose might be to point out the direction in which the boat is moving.

In support of this conclusion, I discovered that the pole was lower than the pilot house, so that the steersman could easily see it. Moreover, the tip was enough higher than the base, so that, from the pilot's position, it must appear to project far out in front of the boat. Moreover, the pilot being near the front of the boat, he would need some such guide as to its direction. Tugboats would also need poles for such a purpose. This hypothesis was so much more probable than the others that I accepted it. I formed the conclusion that the pole was set up for the purpose of showing the pilot the direction in which the boat pointed, to enable him to steer correctly.

3. In washing tumblers [stemless drinking glasses] and placing them mouth downward on a plate, bubbles appeared on the outside of the mouth of the tumblers and then went inside. Why? The presence of bubbles suggest air, which I note must come from inside the tumbler. I see that the soapy water on the plate prevents escape of the air save as it may be caught in bubbles. But why should air leave the tumbler? There was no substance entering to force it out. It must have expanded. It expands by increase of heat or by decrease of pressure, or by both. Could the air have become heated after the tumbler was taken from the hot suds? Clearly not the air that was already entangled in the water. If heated air was the cause, cold air must have entered in transferring the tumblers from the suds to the plate. I test to see if this supposition is true by taking several more tumblers out. Some I shake so as to make sure of entrapping cold air in them. Some I take out holding mouth downward in order to prevent cold air from entering. Bubbles appear on the outside of every one of the former and none of the latter. I must be right in my inference. Air from the outside must have been expanded by the heat of the tumbler, which explains the appearance of the bubbles on the outside.

But why do they then go inside? Cold contracts. The tumbler cooled and also the air inside it. Tension was removed, and hence bubbles appeared inside. To be sure of this, I test by placing a cup on the tumbler while the bubbles are still forming outside. They soon reverse. (pp. 68-71)

Notice how each example of practical reasoning developed from feeling and locating/defining a difficulty—the first two steps of Dewey's strategy. In the first case, the felt difficulty originated from a conflict between conditions at hand and a desired result, the difference between an end and the means for reaching it. In the second case, it was "the incompatibility of a suggested and (temporarily) accepted belief that the pole was a flagpole with certain other facts" (p. 73). And in the third, the provocation occurred because "an observer trained to the idea of natural laws or uniformities finds something odd or exceptional in the behavior of the bubbles" (p. 73). Note also how the reasoning evolved somewhat unpredictably from there as various means-ends thinking patterns took control to suggest possible explanations (Step 3), consider the merit of each (Step 4), and test implications against circumstances at hand (Step 5). This development was traceable but perhaps not predictable from the steps, which served to mark the progression of the problem-solution cycle.

The implication of this analysis is that we all think like this when we solve problems, as the research on human problem solving conducted by Newell and Simon (1972) seems to indicate. These researchers observed people solve a variety of complex problems and identified the steps common to their solution strategies. These steps were

1. Identifying a discrepancy between the goal state of a solved problem and the actual state

2. Searching for an operation to reduce that discrepancy

3. Applying that operator to reduce the discrepancy

4. Returning to Step 1 to repeat the process until the actual state equaled the goal state

Newell and Simon then programmed computers to follow this human-generated strategy in order to find solutions to complex problems in chess, memory, learning, physics engineering, education, rule induction, concept formation, perception, and understanding (pp. 661-784). Simon (1989) described the program responsible for these simulations as follows:

> A problem is defined for GPS [General Problem Solver] by giving it a starting situation and a goal situation (or a test for determining whether the goal has been reached), together with a set of operators that may be used, separately or severally, to transform the starting situation into the goal situation by a sequence of successive applications. Means-ends analysis is the technique used by GPS to decide which operator to apply next:
>
> 1. It compares current situation with goal situation to detect one or more differences between them.
>
> 2. It retrieves from memory an operator that is associated with a difference it has found (i.e., an operator that has the usual effect of reducing differences of this kind).
>
> 3. It applies the operator or, if it is not applicable in the current situation, [Step 4] sets up the new goal of creating the conditions that will make it applicable. (p. 36)

The function of Step 4 of the program is to break complex problems into successively smaller discrepancy problems until an operator is found that eliminates the difference. Then the program works backward through the means-ends chain, eliminating one discrepancy at a time until the actual state equals the goal state to solve the original problem. Newell and Simon (1972) illustrated the everyday reasoning simulated by this program in the following scenario:

> I want to take my son to nursery school. What's the difference between what I have and what I want? One of distance. What changes distance? My automobile. My automobile won't work. What is needed to make it work: A new battery. What has new batteries? An auto repair shop. I want the repair shop to put in a new battery but the shop doesn't know I need one. What is the difficulty? One of communication. What allows communication? Telephone . . . and so on. (p. 416)

This model of reflective problem solving also appears in academic textbooks. Deborah Stone's *Policy Paradox and Political Reason* (1988), for example, uses it to structure the policy-making process:

> The broad architecture of the book takes its shape from the notion of a policy issue implied in the rationality project: We have a goal; we have a problem, which is a discrepancy between the goal and reality; and we seek a solution to erase the discrepancy. Accordingly, any issue can be defined in the following formula:
>
> 1. Something is good, worthwhile, or desirable.
> 2. We don't have it or enough of it.
> 3. How can we accomplish it or attain more of it?
>
> Step 1 is the goal; Step 2 is the problem; Step 3 is the range of possible solutions. A concrete example might look like this:
>
> 1. All citizens should be able to read so that they can have a good life as individuals and can participate fully in society.
> 2. Sixty million adults cannot read beyond the fourth-grade level.
> 3. The government could fund adult literacy programs, or promote research and demonstration programs for teaching reading in the schools, or require a reading test as a condition for obtaining a driver's license, or do any number of plausible or ridiculous things.
>
> There are variations on this basic formula, but they all involve the same three elements of goal, problem, and solution. (p. 8)

Table 1.2 compares constructive theorizing with the practical reasoning described by Dewey, Newel, and Simon. Note how all three strategies begin with a discrepancy condition that provokes means-ends reasoning. Dewey's discrepancy condition provokes a search for an efficient way to get to a meeting (first problem), a search for the purpose of a pole on the bow of a boat (second problem), and a search for the cause of bubbles forming on a tumbler (third problem). Newell and Simon's discrepancy condition provokes a search for a way to get a child to preschool. In both cases, practical reasoning is *a means* of changing a condition of not knowing something to a condition of knowing it.

Theorizing as Self-Regulated Learning

A third view of constructive theorizing is that it regulates learning about different ways of adjusting to unusual circumstances. People use it to direct their

TABLE 1.2

Comparing Practical and Means-Ends Reasoning
With Constructive Theorizing

Dewey's Practical Reasoning[a]	Simon's Means-Ends Reasoning[b]	Constructive Theorizing
1. Define and locate a felt difficulty.	1. Compare a current situation with a goal situation to detect one or more differences between them.	1. Define the problem as a discrepancy between knowing and not knowing the facts, values, or actions associated with a circumstance.
2. Suggest a possible solution.	2. Find an operator associated with these differences that has the effect of reducing them.	2. Find reasons to explain these discrepancies between knowing and not knowing.
3. Develop reasons for the solution.	3. Apply the operator.	3. Evaluate the credibility and worth of the reasons and explanation.
4. Conduct further observations and experiments to test the solution and then accept or reject the solution.	4. Return to Step 1.	4. Adjust existing beliefs by repeating Steps 1 through 3.

a. Dewey (1910/1991, p. 72).
b. Simon (1989, p. 36).

thoughts and actions toward improved beliefs about how things work, how they ought to work, and what should be done about them. An event that attracts attention and motivates a search for reasons and explanations raises the expectation that holding credible and valuable beliefs about the event will improve one's adjustments. Hence, strategies like constructive theorizing, problem solving, and practical reasoning are a *means* of improving those outcomes.

This is also the assumption used to develop various adaptability models described by theorists like Wiener (1948), Ashby (1960), Miller, Galanter, and Pribram (1960), Annett (1969), and Powers (1973). They postulate that all organisms adjust to discrepancy conditions provoked by environmental disturbances, a view reflected in self-directed learning and adjustment models in the social sciences. In psychology, for example, Jackson and Boag (1981) developed a model of self-regulation to describe how individuals with mental retardation learn to self-monitor and compare results with a standard in order to make appropriate adjustments. Kanfer and Hagerman (1981) developed a model focusing on the discrepancies between results and self-assessments that motivate people with depression to cope with their circumstances. And Jeffrey and Berger (1982) constructed a model to show how individuals regulate the emotional reactions to unpleasant events by monitoring their behaviors to detect discrepancies with expectations.

In educational applications, Zimmerman, Bonner, and Kovach (1996) claimed that self-regulated learning is learning that is motivated by "cognitive and emotional reactions to self-monitored outcomes of one's learning, such as heightened attention following a failure" (p. 140). The cycle of regulated learning that they describe has four states: (a) self-monitoring and evaluation to detect discrepancies between expectations and results, (b) planning and goal setting to reduce discrepancies, (c) strategy implementation and monitoring to follow through on plans to meet goals, and (d) strategic-outcome monitoring of results. And in special education, Mithaug, Wehmeyer, Agran, Martin, and Palmer (1998) described a model of self-regulated learning that engages students by teaching them to ask themselves three sets of questions. One set identifies what they want to learn, another directs them to take action to learn what they don't know, and a third set encourages evaluations and adjustments of subsequent learning to finish finding out what they don't know.

All these models have similar regulatory components: (a) a discrepancy condition, (b) expectations to eliminate it, (c) choices and actions to make specific reductions, and (d) comparison of results with expectations to direct subsequent adjustments in expectations, choices, and actions (Mithaug, 1993, pp. 43-62). Perhaps you can detect the models' similarities to four-step problem solving: Define the problem (the discrepancy condition), search for solutions (set expectations to reduce the condition), implement a solution (make choices and actions to meet expectations), and evaluate solutions (adjust to result-expectations comparison).

Dewey's analysis expands our understanding of this strategy by explaining the role of inductive and deductive thinking. The following passage shows how induction finds solutions (Step 2) and how deduction tests them (Step 3):

> This more systematic thinking is, however, like the cruder forms in its double movement, the movement *toward* the suggestion or hypothesis [from Step 1 to Step 2] and the movement *back* to facts [from Step 3 to Step 4]. The difference is in the greater conscious care with which each phase of the process is per-

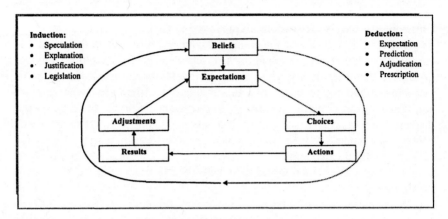

FIGURE 1.1. Constructive Theorizing

formed. *The conditions under which suggestions are allowed to spring up and develop are regulated.* Hasty acceptance of any idea that is plausible, that seems to solve the difficulty, is changed into a conditional acceptance pending further inquiry. The idea is accepted as a *working hypothesis,* as something to guide investigation and bring to light new facts, not as a final conclusion. When pains are taken to make each aspect of the movement as accurate as possible, the movement toward building up the idea is known as *inductive discovery* (*induction* in short); the movement toward developing, applying, and testing, as *deductive proof* (*deduction,* for short).

While induction moves from fragmentary details (or particulars) to a connected view of a situation (universal) [Steps 1 and 2], deduction begins with the latter and works back again to particulars, connecting them and binding them together [Steps 3 and 4]. The inductive movement is toward *discovery* of a binding principle [Step 2], the deductive toward its *testing*—confirming, refuting, modifying it on the basis of its capacity to interpret isolated details into a unified experience [Step 3]. So far as we conduct each of these processes in the light of the other, we get valid discovery or verified critical thinking [italics added]. (Dewey, 1910/1991, pp. 81-82)

Figure 1.1 illustrates this thinking. Its essential factors are beliefs, expectations, choices, actions, and results. The term *induction* describes the process of speculating, explaining, justifying, and legislating, and the term *deduction* describes the process of expecting, predicting, adjudicating, and prescribing.

Deduction occurs when you derive expectations from beliefs, make choices based upon expectations, and then act in consonance with your choices. By regulating these thought processes, you deduce actions from beliefs via the expectation-choice route. You deduce expectations from beliefs, choices from expectations, and then actions from choices. Induction, by contrast, occurs when you compare results with expectations and speculate about reasons for correspondence or lack thereof. You regulate these thoughts by inducing reasons that help you understand a circumstance or result. When the reasons and explanation are consistent with circumstances, you know what to expect in the future.

Regulating inductive and deductive reasoning allows you to think about the past in order to adjust in the present. It is continuous. Deduction leads your thinking to induction, and induction leads it back to deduction. The result is a confirmed or revised belief—the consequence of reconciling a result with an expectation. Figure 1.1 illustrates. The half circle formed by the broken line emanating from the right side of the belief box and ending at the bottom of the figure depicts deductive links between beliefs, expectations, choices, and actions. The terms that describe the process are *expecting, predicting, adjudicating,* and *prescribing.* If you believe X to be credible and valuable, you *expect* Y to happen, *predict* that Y will happen, *adjudicate* the significance of Y's happening, or *prescribe* that Y ought to happen.

During empirical theorizing, for example, a *prediction* about what choices and actions will produce a given outcome is based on a theory about how the world actually functions. During moral theorizing, a *judgment* that a circumstance is good or bad or right or wrong is based on a theory about how things ought to function. During policy theorizing, a *prescription* about what choices and actions ought to occur is based upon a theory about what events should change.

The circle formed by the solid line beginning at the bottom of Figure 1.1 and ending on the left side of the belief box depicts links between results and belief adjustments. The terms that describe the induction of reasons from results include *speculating, explaining, justifying,* and *legislating.* When you obtain a result Y, you *speculate* to produce reasons for Y, *explain* Y with reasons that are consistent with an empirical theory, *justify* Y with reasons that are consistent with a new or an existing moral theory, or *legislate* (enact) Y with reasons that are consistent with a policy theory.

During empirical theorizing, for example, you *explain* an adjustment with the reasons induced from a result. During moral theorizing, you *justify* the adjustment with the reasons induced from a result. During policy theorizing, you *legislate* an adjustment based on reasons induced from a result. In each case, you induce reasons from a result by speculating about causes (for empirical theorizing), about responsibilities (for moral theorizing), or about rules (for policy theorizing). Induction, in summary, is an accounting of the result through a reconciliation between an event or circumstance and an expectation or belief. During empirical theorizing, the result is a new explanation. During moral theorizing, the result is a new justification. During policy theorizing, the result is a new prescription or new rule.

TABLE 1.3

Comparing Self-Regulation and Dewey's Inductive and Deductive Thinking
With Constructive Theorizing

Self-Regulation[a]	Dewey's Induction and Deduction[b]	Constructive Theorizing
1. Discrepancy	1. Discrepancy	1. Discrepancy
2. Expectations to reduce discrepancy	2. Induction to find solutions	2. Induction to construct a theory
3. Choices and actions based on expectations	3. Deduction to test solutions	3. Deduction to evaluate credibility and value of the theory
4. Getting results of actions; adjustment by returning to 1	4. Return to 1	4. Adjustment of other beliefs inconsistent with theory (return to 1)

a. Mithaug (1993, pp. 50-61).
b. Dewey (1910/1991, pp. 81-100).

Table 1.3 presents this view of constructive theorizing as a type of self-regulated learning and as a combination of deductive and inductive thinking. As you can see by comparing the steps in each strategy, the three are logically equivalent.

THEORIZING AND THE UNCOMMON OUTCOME

This ends the analysis of similarities between constructive theorizing and thinking strategies like problem solving, practical reasoning, and self-regulated learning. Now let us turn to how constructive theorizing is different from these strategies. Let us consider the results it produces. Constructive theorizing always produces a theory. It produces an empirical theory to explain circumstances, a moral theory to judge circumstances, and a policy theory to prescribe actions on circumstances. It produces theories that are credible and valuable enough to be adopted and used by others. It uses the criteria of coherence, validity, and verifiability to judge a theory's credibility and the criteria of significance, scope, and utility criteria to judge a theory's worth. Last, the strategy never produces a final solution to problems of not knowing. Hence, the theories it produces are always subject to challenge by new circumstances or by new theorizing that produces more credible or valuable theories. These are the distinctive features of constructive theorizing.

This section illustrates these characteristics by using four-step theorizing to account for an unusual circumstance you may recognize. Reason along with me as we attempt to understand why Casey Martin, a disabled golfer, requested to use a golf cart during a Professional Golf Association (PGA) tournament. When I read about his request in a newspaper article, I thought it was unusual for two reasons. First, the PGA has rules requiring all competitors to walk from hole to hole. Second, Casey Martin won the tournament using the cart. This provoked me to ask the following questions: Why did this happen? Should it have happened? What should be done about it, if anything? We will address each question in turn.

Empirical Theorizing: Why Did It Happen?

The question "Why did Casey Martin request a golf cart during a PGA tournament?" is *empirical* because it asks about the facts or circumstances surrounding Martin's request. The question suggests a discrepancy between what we know about riding carts in PGA tournaments—the known facts—and what we don't know about Casey Martin's request for a cart—the facts or circumstances not yet known. This discrepancy condition provokes a search for reasons to explain what we don't know. The search ends after we evaluate the credibility and worth of the explanation we construct and then decide if we should adopt it and adjust other beliefs about golf tournaments that are inconsistent with this one.

Step 1: Define the Discrepancy

The *New York Times* article on Casey Martin's victory (Nobles, 1997) indicated that Martin rode a cart in the Nike tournament because his physical disability prevented him from walking long distances. Martin has Klippel-Trenaunay-Weber syndrome, a congenital circulatory disorder that causes severe swelling in his right leg. The condition worsens when he walks the 5 miles of an 18-hole course. The article indicated that although Martin had been permitted to use a cart in tournaments sponsored by the National Collegiate Athletic Association, a PGA tournament rule states that "players and caddies shall not use automotive transportation" (Nobles, 1997, p. C1). This is the discrepancy requiring resolution. It is the difference between knowing that a PGA rule prohibits the use of carts and not knowing why Casey Martin requested the use of a cart during a PGA tournament.

Step 2: Find Reasons

Further investigation indicated that the following facts were also associated with this unusual event:

- As a student at Stanford University, Martin was an outstanding golfer, as was his roommate, Tiger Woods.

- At that time, the National Collegiate Athletic Association permitted him to use a cart during tournament play.

- At the 1994 Pac-10 golf championships, which also enforce the rule against use of golf carts, the coaches voted unanimously to let Martin ride in order to compete (Wiswall, 1998).

- The PGA permits use of carts in tournament play on the Senior Tour, which is for people over age 50.

- The PGA also permits the use of golf carts to speed play during the first two phases of its annual qualifying tournament (Sandomir, 1998a).

- The use of new technology affects many sports: The oversize racquet affects the game of tennis, the designated hitter and artificial grass affect the game of baseball, allowing receivers to wear gloves affects football, and Big Berthas increase driving distance for many professional golfers (Berkow, 1998).

- At present, the circulation in Martin's leg has deteriorated to the extent that it is at risk for fracture and amputation should he continue to walk.

- Martin cannot compete in PGA tournaments if he is required to walk.

On the basis of these facts, what is your explanation for why Casey Martin requested a cart during tournament play? The explanation I constructed is presented below. Compare your explanation with mine.

Empirical Theory About Using Golf Carts

1. Improvements in equipment technology have increased the capacity of many athletes to compete successfully in various sports.

2. Some of these technological improvements have made these sporting events accessible to people who otherwise would have been unable to participate.

3. The golf cart has made golfing accessible to people with mobility disabilities who otherwise would have been unable to participate due to the long distances between holes.

4. Given that use of golf carts is an option for all players at most courses and in many amateur and professional tournaments, there is an increased probability

that individuals who cannot walk the course will use a golf cart so that they can compete in these tournaments.

5. Therefore, golfers with mobility disabilities who can play competitive golf are likely to request the use of a golf cart so that they can participate in tournament play.

Step 3: Evaluate Credibility and Value

Now let us evaluate the theory. (You can evaluate your theory at the same time.) Does it explain why Casey Martin requested an exemption from the PGA rule banning cart use during tournament play? Do his circumstances fit those specified in this theory? They appear to fit in that Martin is a competitive golfer whose disability prevents him from walking long distances. He also used a golf cart in other tournaments and was competitive enough to win. But is this a credible and valuable explanation for why he requested the cart this time? Let's find out.

First, evaluate the theory's credibility by considering its coherence, validity, and verifiability. The theory is *coherent* to the extent that its propositions contribute to a logical explanation for why Martin requested a cart. Proposition 1 claims that developments in sporting technology have improved the ability of many athletes to compete successfully in their sports, and Proposition 2 asserts that some of these improvements have made sporting contests accessible to people who would otherwise be unable to compete. Proposition 3 claims that the advent of the golf cart is an example of how sporting technology has made golf tournaments more accessible. Proposition 4 argues that cart usage is commonplace in amateur and professional tournaments and that it increases the probability that people with difficulty walking will use carts to play. Proposition 5 concludes that people with mobility disabilities who are competitive golfers are among those who are likely to request the use of a cart during tournament play.

Does this argument appear to be *coherent* to you? Are any of the propositions irrelevant to the argument or incompatible with each other? Is the argument *valid*? Do the first four propositions lead to the prediction in Proposition 5 that people with disabilities who play competitive golf are likely to request a cart during tournament play? In other words, does the conclusion in Proposition 5 follow from Propositions 1 through 4? If so, then the conclusion in Proposition 5 is likely to be true only if all the other propositions are true.

Finally, ask if the theory is *verifiable*. Consider whether there are tests or existing information to support or refute the five propositions. Could you test the theory directly, for example, by recording the number of cart requests made by players with mobility disabilities during tournament play?

Now let us examine the theory's worth. Is it a significant, comprehensive, and useful explanation for why Casey Martin requested to ride a cart in the tournament? The theory is *significant* if it explains all of the effects of technological improvements on participation in sports. Does it do all of this? Perhaps not, for there are many technological changes influencing sports that have nothing to do with accessibility or people with mobility disabilities. Examples include the use of protective gear to prevent injury in contact sports and the use of various training devices and procedures to enhance performance. Do these considerations limit the theory's significance?

Next, we consider the theory's *scope.* Does it explain a full range of accessibility circumstances caused by these new technologies? Or does the theory apply only to those involving golf carts and people with mobility disabilities? On this score, the theory appears to be somewhat limited.

Finally, we ask if the theory is *useful.* Do its predictions yield secondary benefits for anyone? One obvious benefit is that tournament officials and sponsors will be aware of the needs of people with disabilities and their requests for carts during amateur and professional tournaments. This may help them accommodate these requests in ways that minimize disruptions to the game. Another possible benefit is that golfers with mobility disabilities who hold this belief will feel empowered to request relief from the must-walk rule in order to compete, as Martin did. Finally, as more people adopt this belief, opportunities may increase for all athletes with disabilities to request rule changes to accommodate their needs.

Step 4: Adjust Beliefs

Do you think this theory is credible and valuable enough to adopt? If it is, do you hold other beliefs that are inconsistent with this view? As you consider your answers, remember that acceptance of this theory does not mean that you *approve* of Martin's request for relief from the PGA must-walk rule. It only means that you believe this theory offers a good explanation for why Martin requested a cart. To consider whether Martin's request should be honored, we must find out if it was right for him to request a cart given that a PGA rule prohibits any player from using carts during tournament play.

Moral Theorizing:
How Should We Judge It?

Moral theorizing will help us solve this problem of not knowing if it is right for some golfers to ride carts while others walk. This is a moral question because the exception to the must-walk rule could unfairly affect nondisabled players. To find out if does, let us use the same four steps of constructive theorizing that answered the empirical question about why Casey Martin requested a cart.

Step 1: Define the Discrepancy

Begin by considering some of the reactions from other players about Martin's cart use during tournament play. Brad Faxon said, "The guy [Martin] is a great player, and he deserves all the accolades, but I don't see guys in the N.F.L. who have knee injuries getting mopeds" and "I didn't see Jose Maria Olazabal getting a cart when he was hurt. Where do you draw the line? What if a guy plays three rounds, then gets hurt? Can he take a cart on the fourth round? There are too many scenarios" (quoted in Nobles, 1997, p. C3). Tiger Woods, Martin's roommate at Stanford, said:

> When Casey played at Stanford, he could play 36 holes, but he was in a lot of pain, excruciating pain. . . . Now his leg has deteriorated to the point where he can't walk. As a friend, I'd love to see him have a cart. But from a playing standpoint, is it an advantage? It could be. If it's 100 degrees in Memphis, does it help to ride? (quoted in Nobles, 1997, p. C3)

Mark Calcavecchia, another PGA winner, disagrees:

> Originally, I didn't think he should be allowed to ride. . . . But obviously, if he's as good a player as he is, if he's good enough to win on the Nike Tour, I think he should be allowed to come out here, see what happens, and let it rip. (quoted in Nobles, 1997, p. C3)

As you can see, these questions reflect a concern about fairness. And, as Dave Anderson (1998) has suggested, what is fair for everyone is unclear:

> Over the years, most golf debates have involved the height of the rough, the speed of the greens and whether a short putt is a gimmie.
> But by invoking the Americans with Disabilities Act in his suit, Martin has created a human debate: does riding carts give a tournament golfer an unfair advantage over those who must walk? (p. C1)

The fairness problem appears to have two parts. One is whether riding a cart gives Martin an unfair advantage over players who walk. The other, as suggested by the Americans with Disabilities Act, is whether the must-walk rule discriminates against people with mobility disabilities. These issues define the discrepancy between knowing it is unfair to prevent Martin from competing in golf because of his mobility disability and not knowing if Martin's use of a cart is unfair to those prohibited from using a cart. It is the problem that additional theorizing will attempt to solve.

Step 2: Find Reasons

In the search for reasons to resolve this discrepancy, let us consider some of the arguments for and against Martin's request. One side claims that allowing Martin to use a cart is fair to other golfers if it does not create an advantage for him to win tournaments. Dave Anderson (1998) argued that when Martin won the PGA event, "The cart didn't hit any of Martin's winning shots. The cart didn't putt for him. The cart didn't think for him. And if Martin doesn't hit as many good shots this weekend, it won't be the cart's fault" (p. C1).

The other side claims that allowing Martin to use a cart will give him an "endurance" advantage. Tim Finchem, the PGA Tour commissioner, stated that "endurance is a part of our sport" and that "walking has been an integral part of the competition on all Tours and has been uniformly recognized as an integral part of the competition by all the major bodies in golf for a long, long time" (quoted in Chambers, 1998b, p. C7). Jack Nicklaus agreed: "I am concerned for Casey Martin; however, I very much believe that to play the sport, you have to have the physical part of it, too." He asserted:

> If I were allowed to use a cart, I would be able to compete much better on the
> regular tour, simply because my hip just wears out on me. That is a disability,
> but I am not going to ride a cart, nor have I ridden a cart on the Senior Tour yet.
> (quoted in Brown, 1998, p. C2)

Finally, the PGA argued that the must-walk rule is a fundamental part of the game and that changing that rule would alter it unjustifiably.

During court testimony, however, the following facts were presented:

- Dr. Gary King's testimony during Martin's federal lawsuit against the PGA indicated that walking is "not a particularly lot of exertion, especially because it's spread out over four or five hours" and that a round of golf would expend approximately 500 calories, which is "nutritionally less than a Big Mac" (quoted in Sandomir, 1998d, p. C4).

- Casey Martin is an "inefficient walker" in that he uses more energy to walk than the average person. Walking is a significant disadvantage.

- Martin's court demonstration showed that when he stands on his disabled leg, "blood settles in hardened black-and-blue patches below a damaged knee that swells instantly. Only when he laid down did blood return via constricted veins" (Sandomir, 1998a, p. C4).

■ No golf book indicates that walking is fundamental to golf, and no evidence indicates that use of a golf cart increases the chance of winning (Sandomir, 1998a).

If we use these facts to construct a theory of fairness, we might argue along the lines of the following moral theory that explains why tournaments that prohibit golf cart use are unfair to competitors with mobility disabilities:

A Moral Theory About Using Golf Carts

1. Open invitations to compete in a sporting event are fair to the extent that all people who want to participate are allowed to compete, regardless of their performance on criteria that are irrelevant to winning the event.

2. Using a cart to get from hole to hole is irrelevant to winning in tournament golf.

3. Individuals whose physical disabilities prevent them from getting from hole to hole by walking cannot participate in tournament golf without use of a golf cart.

4. Therefore, golf tournaments that deny individuals with disabilities the use of a golf cart are unfair because they exclude those persons from tournament play on criteria that are irrelevant to winning the game.

Step 3: Evaluate Credibility and Value

Is this a credible and valuable explanation for judging golf tournaments that deny carts to golfers with mobility disabilities? The argument is credible to the extent that it is coherent, valid, and verifiable. Consider *coherence* first. Do the propositions offer a logical argument? To answer, consider each in turn. Proposition 1 defines the condition of fairness in sporting events that are open to all comers, and Propositions 2 and 3 identify conditions that are consistent with fairness as defined in Proposition 1: Cart riding is irrelevant to winning at golf, and people with disabilities need to ride carts to participate in open competitions. Now see if the argument is *valid* by noting whether the conclusion in Proposition 4 follows from the premises in Propositions 1 through 3. If it does, then the truth of those propositions will affect the truth of the conclusion. If they are true, the conclusion is likely to be true, and if any are false, the conclusion is false. You can test this by assuming one of the propositions to be false while arguing the conclusion to be true. Can you do this? If you can, the argument is invalid because if there is an inconsistency or irrelevancy among the propositions, then you can argue the conclusion to be true even though the premises are false.

Now ask if the theory is *verifiable.* Can you think of any evidence that would support or refute the propositions? One possibility might be to check the definition in Proposition 1 to see if it is acceptable to people associated with open competitions. Another would be to find out if walking from hole to hole determines winners and losers in those tournaments. Also, you could determine if other people with mobility disabilities can walk during tournament play and still compete on a par with nondisabled golfers. Do you think information like this is sufficient to verify or refute the theory?

To evaluate the theory's value, ask if it presents a significant, comprehensive, and useful explanation for why tournaments that deny carts to people with mobility disabilities are unfair. The theory is *significant* if it can account for all factors of fairness affecting people with mobility disabilities who cannot compete due to circumstances that are irrelevant to winning the game. Can it? What about people who have back problems and also have difficulty walking from hole to hole? Do they deserve a cart for the same reasons Casey Martin deserves one? According to the theory, they do if their problem constitutes a mobility disability. Now ask about people with other types of disabilities. Do people who are blind qualify as having a mobility disability that would justify their being driven in a cart from hole to hole? Could they ask to use a Seeing Eye dog instead? Again, the theory may apply. If it does, its significance is enhanced. The more variation in accessibility circumstances covered by the fairness explanation, the more significant the theory is.

To evaluate the theory's *scope,* ask if it can be used to judge the fairness of other aspects of the game that are also irrelevant to winning or losing. For example, does this theory cover the rule that all participants wear trousers rather than shorts during tournament play? Does it cover the rule that players must finish playing each hole within a given time period or the rule that requires players to keep track of their own scores by signing their cards at the end of each round? Do you think rules like these prevent players from playing their best during tournaments? Does this theory cover their circumstances? Probably not, because it says nothing about rules governing competition operations that are unrelated to winning or losing. Does this limit its scope?

Last, ask yourself if the theory is *useful.* Ask if holding this belief offers secondary benefits for anyone. To stimulate thinking, consider what might happen if all members of the golfing community adopted this theory. This could have the effect of settling the debate about a disabled golfer's right to use a cart during tournament play. This in turn would give officials enforcing the rules of the game a basis for honoring a disabled golfer's request for a cart. It would also inform the golfing community that accommodations would be available to any person whose disability prevented efficient walking during competitive play. Are these benefits sufficient to deem the theory useful?

Step 4: Adjust Beliefs

The last step in this episode of moral theorizing is to decide if the theory is credible and valuable enough for you to adopt. If it is, try to determine the effect of this adoption on other beliefs you hold about professional golf. Consider this scenario. Assume that you also believe that only able-bodied people play professional sports, that golf is a professional sport, and therefore that only able-bodied people should play the game. If you decided to adopt the theory with a mind-set like this, you would probably have major belief adjustments to make. Do you have any ideas how you might proceed? You could consider changing the first belief that only able-bodied people play professional sports. This would alter the conclusion and eliminate the inconsistency. Or you could argue that golf is different from sports like football where only able-bodied people participate. Of course, professional golfers might object to this view.

I think you probably get the point here. Holding contrary beliefs creates obstacles to adopting a new theory, and these problems must be resolved before you can fully integrate the theory into your system of knowing what to believe.

Policy Theorizing: What Should We Do About It?

Now let us turn to the question of what to do about tournaments that deny golf carts to golfers with mobility disabilities. This is a question of action rather than one of fact or value. It is located at that point in the facts-values-actions nexus where the understanding provided by empirical and moral theories can help determine what should be done. Again, four-step theorizing will find some answers.

Step 1: Define the Discrepancy

The claim that it is unfair for tournaments to deny carts to golfers with mobility disabilities creates a problem of not knowing how to act fairly toward all persons in the game. Should the PGA accept Martin's claim that prohibiting cart use during tournament play unfairly discriminates against him and consequently is in violation of the Americans with Disabilities Act? Or should the PGA reject the claim because it is a private organization and hence exempt from the Americans with Disabilities Act?

This was considered by PGA Tour attorneys, who argued that

> while plaintiff's [Martin's] golf skills and accomplishments may be notable, and perhaps even inspirational, Congress never intended the ADA to require a

private organization such as the PGA Tour to change the rules of its tournaments to accommodate a would-be participant. (quoted in Chambers, 1998b,
p. C7)

According to the PGA Tour commissioner, Time Finchem, this case is about
"whether or not the courts should make the rules of the game or the governing
body of the game should make those rules" (Chambers, 1998b, p. C7). PGA officials believe that changing the no-cart rule for Martin will erode the integrity of
the game by allowing any person with a physical difficulty to challenge its rules.
Richard Sandomir (1998b), who covered the case, quoted officials who said that
"allowing him [Casey Martin] to ride in a cart would change the game and lead
others with ailments to also request carts" (p. C7).

This problem of not knowing what should be done can be defined as a discrepancy *between knowing* that the PGA policy preventing persons like Casey
Martin from competing in tournament golf is unfair *and not knowing* if requiring
the PGA to change its rules is also unfair to the organization and to other golfers
who abide by those rules. If we can find reasons to resolve this discrepancy, perhaps we will also identify what actions are appropriate under the circumstances.

Step 2: Find Reasons

On February 11, 1998, the Federal District Court in Oregon provided some
reasons to resolve this discrepancy. Judge Thomas M. Coffin ruled in favor of
Casey Martin's request to use a cart in PGA tournaments. He said that (a) the
PGA was a public entity and therefore under the jurisdiction of the Americans
with Disabilities Act, (b) walking was not essential for playing tournament golf,
and (c) allowing Casey Martin to use a golf cart would not give him an unfair
advantage. The evidence and testimony supporting this ruling included the
following:

■ The PGA Tour is a public event. Therefore, under the Americans with Disabilities
  Act, the PGA and its rules and policies must not discriminate against persons with
  disabilities. Judge Coffin ruled that the question of whether and how the A.D.A.
  applies to athletic rules does not have different answers depending upon where
  the athletic competition takes place at. It's the same at high school, college, pros,
  the rules are the rules, and it doesn't matter which entity has those rules. (quoted
  in Chambers, 1998a, p. C9)

■ Testimony in the case indicated that the must-walk rule is not as fundamental to
  the game of golf as claimed. Instead, it is "among several 'considerations of competition and local rules' that exist as an addendum to the standard United States
  Golf Association rule book followed by the PGA Tour, the N.C.A.A. and numer-
  ous other golf bodies" (Sandomir, 1998c, p. C7). Moreover, the PGA offered no
  documentation that walking is fundamental to the operations of golf (Sandomir,
  1998b).

■ Although allowing Casey Martin to use a cart because of his mobility disability may set a precedent for allowing other athletes with disabilities to compete in various events, each person must qualify as being disabled under the provision of the Americans with Disabilities Act to take advantage of this opportunity to participate (Chambers, 1998a).

■ Judge Coffin ruled that "Mr. Martin is entitled to his modification because he is disabled. It will not alter what's taking place out there on the course" (quoted in Chambers, 1998a, p. A1).

The following policy theory is based on these findings as well as the reasoning provided by our empirical and moral theories about open competitions in tournament golf.

Policy Theory About Using Golf Carts

1. Discrimination on factors that are irrelevant to one's job responsibilities is unfair.

2. The Americans with Disabilities Act prohibits employment practices that discriminate on disability factors unrelated to one's job responsibilities.

3. Tournament golf is a public event that employs individuals who have the skills to compete.

4. One of the rules of the PGA is that during tournament play all players must walk from hole to hole.

5. Some individuals with mobility disabilities have the skills to play tournament golf but need a golf cart to move from hole to hole.

6. The PGA rules banning the use of golf carts during tournament play discriminate against these individuals on factors that are irrelevant to playing tournament golf.

7. This rule is unfair and in violation of the Americans with Disabilities Act.

8. Therefore, the rule must be set aside for people with mobility disabilities.

Step 3: Evaluate Credibility and Value

Do you think this a credible and valuable theory for prescribing how to act on our empirical and moral theories about cart riding in PGA tournaments? Let us examine the theory's credibility first by deciding if it is a coherent, valid, and verifiable explanation for what should be done.

The explanation appears to be *coherent* in that it is based on three claims:

1. Discrimination based on factors that are irrelevant to job performance is unfair (Proposition 1).

2. Discrimination on the basis of disability is one of those irrelevant factors in employment that is unfair (Proposition 2).

3. PGA golf tournaments are a type of workplace governed by federal anti-discrimination law (Proposition 3).

Propositions 4 through 6 show how the PGA violates this principle of fairness by discriminating against golfers on the basis of disability. Propositions 7 and 8 provide conclusions based on these claims. Can you see how Propositions 4 through 6 develop logically from Propositions 1 through 3? Does this structure make the argument coherent?

Now consider the *validity* of the conclusion in Proposition 8. It is true if the preceding propositions are true, and false if any of those propositions are false. To test this, imagine one of the propositions to be false while trying to argue the conclusion to be true nonetheless. Can you do this? Or does the argument become illogical or meaningless when you do it?

Next, ask if the theory is *verifiable,* if there is a way to test it. One way is to note what happens when other people with disabilities bring similar discrimination claims against the PGA. Will these suits result in decisions similar to Judge Thomas Coffin's ruling, which, in effect, required the PGA to make an exception to the must-walk rule, the conclusion in Proposition 8? Another test is to note what happens when the PGA seeks a reversal of Judge Coffin's decision in the Court of Appeals. Will these results affect the veracity of the theory?

Now consider the theory's worth. Is it a significant, comprehensive, and useful method for deciding what should be done? To be *significant,* the theory's prescription for action must address all questions of not knowing how to be fair to people with mobility disabilities during golf tournaments. Does it? It does if every time a PGA rule unfairly discriminates against a person with a disability, it is set aside, for this is the action the theory prescribes. The PGA must make an exception for that person. Moreover, if this is the only solution ever needed to resolve problems of unfairness, the theory's prescriptions have accounted for all actions taken to correct unfair circumstances. Wouldn't this suggest that the theory is significant?

Next, examine the theory's *scope.* Can the theory solve other types of problems of unfair treatment? Can golfers with chronic back problems use its prescription to request an exemption from the four-round, consecutive-day schedule of play, for example? Can they use the theory to demand that the PGA allow them to finish the tournament in 5 or 6 days? Would this demonstration expand the theory's scope?

Last, ask yourself if the theory is *useful.* Do people who hold it experience secondary benefits? Are they empowered to use it to challenge other rules of the game that they believe discriminate against people with disabling conditions? Do PGA officials use the theory to guide their policies and practices by seeking out and eliminating discriminatory rules that are irrelevant to the game? Are they willing, because of the theory, to make the game more accessible to all persons?

Do parents encourage their children with mobility disabilities to learn to play the game because of this new view of fairness in tournament golf? Do golf cart manufacturers construct new types of golf carts for people with disabilities according to PGA specifications for tournament play? Do advertisers market products to take advantage of the positive imagery associated with underdogs like Casey Martin who win the right to play competitive golf against all odds (Chambers, 1998b)? Would answers to questions like these help you decide about the usefulness of this new policy theory?

Step 4: Adjust Beliefs

To end this demonstration of constructive theorizing, ask yourself if this policy theory is credible and valuable enough to adopt. Also ask if other beliefs you hold about professional sports do not contradict this one. If, for example, you believe that people in professional sports are the best athletes in the world and that disabled people cannot compete with them due to their physical infirmities, then you may experience difficulty accepting this view. You may have to adjust too many other beliefs about professional sports. Belief adjustment will be easier, of course, if you think all people deserve a fair chance to compete, regardless of their physical circumstances. Even then, you may feel the need to theorize anew in order to accept the idea that a person can be a great athlete *and* have a disability.

WHAT'S NEXT

One goal of this chapter was to identify similarities between four-step theorizing and routine thinking strategies like problem solving, practical reasoning, and self-regulated learning. Another goal was to identify differences as well. The chapter highlighted the latter by using constructive theorizing to explain why Casey Martin requested a golf cart during tournament play. It showed that unlike problem solving, practical reasoning, or self-regulated learning, constructive theorizing produces theories about how things work, how they ought to work, and what to do about them. The chapter also showed that unlike those strategies, constructive theorizing always evaluates its results, even though those judgments never yield final evaluations of a theory's credibility or worth. The theories constructed in this chapter are like this. At best, they are temporary explanations. Any new circumstance that is inconsistent with their claims can challenge their credibility or value.

This is the nature of all theories constructed by the method. They are good for adoption and use only to the extent that they are more credible and more valuable than their alternatives. In fact, a basic premise of this strategy is that every person prefers to hold beliefs that are credible and valuable when possible. Consequently, when people discover that their beliefs lack credibility and value, they should try replacing them with beliefs that are more credible and more valuable. You may disagree with this premise because you don't think it matters if your own beliefs are credible or valuable. After all, they are *your beliefs,* and as long as you are comfortable with them, nothing else matters. Moreover, it is simply impractical to spend much time worrying about such things.

In the next chapter, I offer a counterargument and corresponding theory for why holding only credible and valuable beliefs benefits everyone, including you. The crux of this argument is that this type of beliefs will improve your adjustments and hence your prospects for getting what you need and want in life. This is the same argument that William James (1907/1991) put forth in his pragmatic theory of knowledge, which is that credible and valuable beliefs will make a positive difference in your life and that therefore you should try to hold them when you can. The chapter uses four-step theorizing to construct a theory of credible and valuable beliefs that explains and justifies this claim. It also shows how six criteria for evaluating credibility and value will help you decide which beliefs to hold and which beliefs to improve or replace.

MY VIEW OF TRUTH

Many people believe that a quest for knowledge and understanding is also a search for truth. In this book, I avoid this claim, even though theorizing can, on occasion, yield results that appear to reflect a fundamental truth. Instead of calling those outcomes "true" in that sense, I call them credible and valuable. Then I place them on the continuum of tentative judgment, where their credibility and value can wax or wane as new information and unexpected circumstance emerge to support or refute.

So on the question of ultimate truth I am agnostic. Perhaps there is final truth residing in some types of knowledge, as Edward Wilson (1998) has claimed, or perhaps there are only contingent truths in all types of knowledge, as Richard Rorty (1998) has claimed. I don't know. But I do know that the tiny truths that we construct routinely in various quests to understand can be judged to be more or less credible in accordance with Wilson's standards of knowing and to be more or less valuable in accordance with Rorty's standards for knowing. Moreover, when we make these judgments about credibility and worth, we gain incrementally in our knowledge about the adjustments that will improve our empirical, moral, and political circumstances.

Constructing Credible and Valuable Beliefs

The practical argument for preferring credible and valuable beliefs is that they give predictability to life by connecting the past with the present and by linking the present with the future. They give meaning and substance to daily adjustments by helping us understand our circumstances so we can act on them effectively. They are, as William James claimed in *Pragmatism* (1907/1991), *instruments* for making a difference in one's life:

> "Truth" in our ideas and beliefs means the same thing that it means in science. It means . . . nothing but this, *that ideas (which themselves are but parts of our experience) become true just in so far as they help us to get into satisfactory relations with other parts of our experience,* to summarize them and get about among them by conceptual short-cuts instead of following the interminable succession of particular phenomena. Any idea upon which we can ride, so to speak; any idea that will carry us prosperously from any one part of our experience to any other part, linking things satisfactorily, working securely, simplifying, saving labor, is true for just so much, true in the so far forth, true *instrumentally*. (p. 28)

Of course, beliefs can also cause distress by failing to tell us what to expect and how to benefit from what we know. When this happens, we lose confidence in our choices and actions. Suddenly, we are motivated to resolve discrepancies between our expectations and our circumstances because by knowing what to believe we know how to adjust to those circumstances.

In this chapter, I use four-step theorizing to construct a theory that supports the belief that it is in your interest to hold credible and valuable beliefs. The chapter investigates the merits of the argument that (a) everyone wants to adjust successfully to his or her circumstances, (b) people who hold beliefs that are credible and valuable are more likely to adjust successfully to their circumstances than people who hold suspect and worthless beliefs, and (c) therefore everyone should want to hold only those beliefs that are credible and valuable.

We will begin by assuming the first statement to be true, that everyone wants to adjust successfully to his or her circumstances. From here we will attempt to explain why the second and third statements are also true. To account for the second claim, we will find out why credible and valuable beliefs are necessary for successful adjustments. To support the third claim, we will find out why people prefer credible and valuable beliefs to beliefs that are credible but not valuable, beliefs that are valuable but not credible, and beliefs that are neither credible nor valuable.

By the end of the chapter, you will be able to judge the credibility and worth of this theory that it is in your interest to hold only beliefs that are credible and valuable. By then, you will know why evaluating a theory's credibility and worth is essential to knowing how to improve your adjustments. You will also have another example of how four-step theorizing solves a problem of not knowing how things work. In this case, the problem is one of not knowing why credible and valuable beliefs help you improve your adjustments.

STEP 1: DEFINE THE DISCREPANCY PROBLEM

The claim that you depend upon beliefs to adjust to various circumstances in life can be explained by noting how beliefs generate expectations that, in turn, guide choices and actions. Consider, for example, the problem of adjusting to the weather. When a belief leads you to expect rain, you carry an umbrella, and when it rains as you expect it will, you use the umbrella to stay dry. On the other hand, when the same belief leads you to expect sunshine, you leave the umbrella home, and when it does not rain as you predicted, you are not burdened by carrying an umbrella. Your belief about the weather tells you when to expect rain and when to expect sunshine, and those expectations, in turn, influence your choices and actions regarding an umbrella. The result is an optimal adjustment. You have an umbrella when it rains, and you are free of it when it does not. Your belief about the weather is supported by a *credible* and *valuable* theory about how the weather works. The theory is credible because it accurately predicts rain and nonrain days. It is valuable because it gives you useful information for staying dry during rainy days and being free of umbrellas during sunshine days. This theory and the belief that it supports are worth keeping because they produce expectations that are consistent with circumstances (they are credible) and because these expectations in turn aid in your adjustments (they are valuable).

This is the basic reason why everyone—including you—should want to hold only beliefs that are credible and valuable. It does not explain, however, why people may also hold beliefs that are not credible or not valuable. Clearly, holding beliefs like these is *inconsistent* with the explanation that it is in everyone's interest to hold only beliefs that are credible *and* valuable. This is the *discrepancy problem* that we will address in this demonstration of constructive theorizing.

Let us begin by defining the problem as a *discrepancy* between the condition of knowing why people hold some beliefs—beliefs that are credible and valuable—and the condition of not knowing why people hold beliefs that lack credibility or that lack value. We already know why people hold beliefs that are credible and valuable. They hold them because these beliefs produce expectations that are consistent with circumstances (they are credible) and because they predict the outcomes of various choices and actions (they are valuable). Let us state this claim about credible and valuable beliefs as follows: "The more often beliefs are consistent with circumstances, the more likely it is that they will become *credible* to the believer; and the more often they can be used to set expectations for choices and actions, the more likely it is that they will become *valuable* to the believer." This is the explanation for why people hold beliefs that are credible and valuable.

Now we come to the problem. This explanation does not account for why people also hold beliefs that are not credible or that are not valuable. This fact appears to be inconsistent with the claim that it is in their interest to hold only credible and valuable beliefs. If credible and valuable beliefs are so much more helpful than other types of beliefs, why do people hold these less desirable beliefs?

To resolve this discrepancy, consider some of the reasons that may change this condition of not knowing to a condition of knowing. In the language of means-ends problem solving (see Chapter 1), this is a problem of reducing the discrepancy between a *goal state* of knowing why people hold all beliefs and an *actual state* of knowing only why people hold beliefs that are credible and valuable. Solving the problem will require a search for reasons to reduce the discrepancy. Once these reasons are known, we can combine them with our knowledge about why people hold beliefs that are credible and valuable to construct a more complete explanation for why people hold all types of beliefs. Hopefully, this will eliminate the difference between the actual state and the goal state.

STEP 2: FIND REASONS

To begin this step, let us consider what happens when beliefs work as expected during an adjustment. They generate expectations for what is likely to occur in a situation, and these expectations guide choices and actions for making an adjustment. In other words, beliefs suggest what to do in that situation. When you take an action that is consistent with a belief, you expect results to be consistent with the expectations derived from it. And when you compare results with that expectation and they match, you are satisfied with your belief. It is credible in that it provided expectations that matched results, and it is valuable in that it guided you toward a successful adjustment. You will probably use the belief again in similar situations. This is what happens when beliefs work as they should.

Reasons

Figure 2.1 illustrates the process. It begins with a belief that generates an expectation that, in turn, influences choices and actions in anticipation of a result. The evaluation that follows determines the match between results and expectations. This captures what you have learned so far—that beliefs influence expectations, which guide choices and actions. It also identifies what you may not have known about the influence of circumstances on beliefs: that *results determine the credibility of beliefs only through an evaluation conducted by the believer.* This is indicated by the arrow connecting the results and evaluation and by the arrow connecting the evaluation and expectations. In other words, a result produced by actions taken by a believer must be evaluated by that believer for him or her to conclude about the credibility of the belief.

This is a new factor for determining how beliefs work during adjustments. Let us state the new reason as follows: *If believers monitor the results of their actions by comparing those outcomes with the expectations generated by their beliefs, they will discover which beliefs are consistent with those circumstances and which are not.* Believers who make these comparisons to evaluate the credibility of their beliefs are more likely to identify inconsistencies between circumstances (results) and beliefs (expectations) than believers who do not. Consequently, they are more likely to hold credible beliefs.

Does this explain why some believers hold beliefs that are valuable but not credible? To find out, consider what happens when believers *fail to evaluate* their beliefs by matching their expectations with circumstances. Will they know which beliefs are credible and which are not? The chances are that they won't. Unless someone tells them their beliefs are suspect, they may hold many beliefs that lack credibility. Moreover, they will continue holding these suspect beliefs because they never check them to find out which ones are false. Their failure to self-monitor explains why some of their beliefs may be valuable but not credible.

This appears to account for one third of the inconsistencies—why people hold beliefs that are valuable but not credible. However, it does not explain why people also may hold beliefs that are credible but not valuable or beliefs that are neither credible nor valuable. To find reasons for these inconsistencies, we must look elsewhere in the adjustment process depicted in Figure 2.1. We must examine the logic links between a belief and a result—the expectations, choices, and actions derived from the belief—because these connections are necessary to evaluate the credibility of the belief.

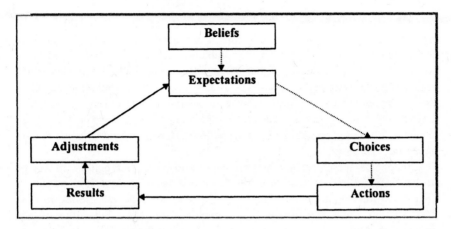

FIGURE 2.1. The Adjustment Process

Examine Figure 2.1 again, and note the broken lines connecting beliefs, expectations, choices, and actions. They represent the following deductive reasoning and conclusion. When an expectation is implied by a belief, a choice is implied by the expectation, and when an action is implied by the choice, *then* a result can be used to verify a belief. These *deductive connections* must be present for the evaluation to occur. Any break in the chain renders the verification test worthless. Hence, all beliefs lacking these links between their expectations and actions—beliefs that lack value, for example—cannot be verified. There are no results that can support or refute a worthless belief (a belief lacking value).

This lack of linkage between beliefs and actions is another reason that people hold beliefs that lack credibility or value. People hold beliefs that are credible but not valuable or beliefs that are neither credible nor valuable because these beliefs are irrelevant to their expectations, choices, and actions. The credibility of these beliefs cannot be verified. Some of them may be credible and others may not. But because believers have no way of knowing which is which, they may hold both types.

This reasoning also explains why adopting a worthless belief because someone tells you that it is credible can perpetuate its acceptance. If you believe what you are told about a belief's credibility, you have no reason to check it yourself. And even if you try, you cannot because the belief is worthless in guiding expectations, choices, and actions. So you hold it simply because people claim it is credible. Now you hold a belief for reasons that are irrelevant to its credibility or worth. But because you lack knowledge of its credibility or because you lack the ability to evaluate and replace it yourself, you are stuck with it. This may also be true of many beliefs that you hold. Because they are worthless, you cannot verify them, and hence *you may never discover* that they lack credibility.

Of course, this is not the problem associated with holding beliefs that are valuable. They guide choices and actions. Consequently, you can always evaluate their credibility by matching results with the expectations that they imply. For these beliefs, the problem of knowing what to believe rests not with the belief but rather with the actions of the believer. Believers who do not monitor results to verify expectations never know whether a belief is credible. Hence, they may hold beliefs that are valuable but not credible due to their failure or inability to evaluate the consequences of what they believe. They may hold *valuable beliefs that lack credibility.*

It appears, therefore, that the problem of knowing which beliefs are worthless is different from that of knowing which beliefs are suspect. It also appears that both problems are due to factors associated with believers. Believers who lack accurate knowledge of their beliefs may hold worthless beliefs that cannot be verified. And believers who lack the ability to improve beliefs may hold suspect beliefs because they do not evaluate their credibility. As a result, these believers may hold beliefs that are *credible but worthless, valuable but suspect,* or *suspect and worthless.*

Explanations

Figure 2.1 identifies the two factors responsible for these outcomes. The first factor, illustrated by the solid line at the bottom left side of the diagram, is the causal relationship between actions, results, and evaluations. Believers who observe this relationship can verify the *credibility* of their beliefs. The second factor, illustrated by the broken line on the right of the diagram, is the logical relationship between beliefs, expectations, choices, and actions. Believers who observe this relationship can judge the *value* of their beliefs.

By keeping this model of deductive and inductive reasoning in mind, perhaps we can solve the problem of not knowing why people hold all types of beliefs. We can claim that one set of reasons explains why people hold beliefs that are credible and valuable and that another set of reasons explains why they hold beliefs that are not credible or not valuable. And by combining the two sets, we can explain why people hold all four types—beliefs that are credible and valuable, beliefs that are credible but not valuable, beliefs that are not credible but are valuable, and beliefs that are neither credible nor valuable.

Translating the first set of reasons into propositions produces the claim that beliefs are credible and valuable to believers to the extent that they (a) are consistent with the circumstances they claim to explain and (b) guide the expectations, choices, and actions of those believers in dealing with those circumstances. Propositions 1 and 2 make these assertions. Proposition 3 concludes that believers benefit from these beliefs by being able to predict the results of their choices and actions, which, by implication, improves their adjustments to those circumstances.

Proposition 1: The more credible a belief, the more often it produces expectations that are consistent with circumstances.

Proposition 2: The more valuable a belief, the more often it produces expectations that guide choices and actions.

Proposition 3: The more credible and valuable a belief, the more likely it is that believers will hold that belief because it guides them to set expectations, make choices, and take actions that produce circumstances that are consistent with the belief.

The second set of reasons explains why rational and prudent people may also hold beliefs that lack credibility or value. It focuses on what believers must do to find out which beliefs are credible and valuable. First, they must be logical when connecting their beliefs with their expectations, choices, and actions. Second, they must be analytical in evaluating the correspondence between their results and expectations. When these conditions are present, believers know which beliefs are credible, which beliefs are valuable, and which beliefs are neither credible nor valuable. Consequently, they will hold only credible and valuable beliefs because (a) they know which beliefs are valuable and which beliefs are credible and (b) they know how to evaluate and improve beliefs that lack credibility or value. Propositions 4 through 6 summarize this explanation for why some believers hold *only* beliefs that are credible and valuable.

Proposition 4: The greater the knowledge of a believer about credible and valuable beliefs, the more likely it is that the believer will derive expectations, choices, and actions from those beliefs and the more often the circumstances resulting from those actions will be consistent with the beliefs.

Proposition 5: The greater the ability of a believer to evaluate and improve the credibility and value of beliefs, the more often that believer will evaluate and improve beliefs that lack credibility or value.

Proposition 6: Believers who have the knowledge and ability to evaluate and improve beliefs are likely to derive expectations from beliefs that are credible and valuable and, as a consequence, are likely to make choices and take actions to produce circumstances that are consistent with their beliefs.

This completes Step 2, which searched for reasons to explain why believers hold all types of beliefs. The explanation was intended to eliminate the discrepancy created by the goal state of knowing why people hold all types of beliefs and the actual state of knowing only why people hold beliefs that are credible and valuable. The first explanation claims that people hold credible and valuable beliefs because (a) these beliefs help them set expectations that predict outcomes that are consistent with the results produced by their choices and actions and (b) this capacity to predict improves their chances of adjusting optimally to their circumstances. The second explanation claims that people hold beliefs that lack credibility, value, or credibility and value because (a) they do not know these beliefs lack credibility or value and (b) they do not have the ability to evaluate and improve or replace beliefs that lack credibility or valuable. Taken together, the explanations imply that when people know that their beliefs lack credibility and value *and* when they are able to improve or replace beliefs that lack credibility or value, they will alter them because making these changes will improve their chances of getting what they need and want in life.

STEP 3: EVALUATE CREDIBILITY AND VALUE

The next step in this demonstration of four-step theorizing evaluates the credibility and value of this theory. To assess the credibility of any new theory, you must decide if it is coherent, valid, and true. To assess its worth, you must determine if the theory is significant, comprehensive, and useful. The credibility criteria evaluate how well the theory accounts for the unusual circumstance, and the worth criteria identify the benefits of holding the theory. Because these assessments are independent of each other, it is possible to judge a theory to be credible and valuable, credible but not valuable, valuable but not credible, or neither credible nor valuable.

Consider, for example, how the criteria differentiate theories that are valuable but not credible. This type of theory can fail the truth test in the following ways: It can fail to provide a coherent set of reasons for its explanation of the unusual circumstance in question; it can fail to offer a conclusion that follows from those reasons; or it can fail to yield predictions that are consistent with the circumstances it purports to explain.

Now consider how the criteria differentiate theories that are credible but not valuable. If a theory is credible but not valuable, it fails the worth test on one of the following: (a) It fails to prescribe solutions that produce substantial reduction in the discrepancy problem (a lack of significance); (b) it fails to solve other types of discrepancy problems (a lack of scope); or (c) it fails to prescribe choices and actions that affect important adjustment circumstances (lack of utility).

When evaluating a theory, you will discover few theories that score uniformly well on all six criteria. The following section presents some of the questions and judgments you will make when deciding whether a theory is sufficiently credible and valuable to adopt. Keep in mind that there are no definitive

TABLE 2.1
A Theory of Credible and Valuable Beliefs

Proposition 1: The more credible a belief, the more often it produces expectations that are consistent with circumstances.

Proposition 2: The more valuable a belief, the more often it produces expectations that guide choices and actions.

Proposition 3: The more credible and valuable a belief, the more likely it is that believers will hold that belief because it guides them to set expectations, make choices, and take actions that produce circumstances that are consistent with the belief.

Proposition 4: The greater the knowledge of a believer about credible and valuable beliefs, the more likely it is that the believer will derive expectations, choices, and actions from those beliefs and the more often the circumstances resulting from those actions will be consistent with beliefs.

Proposition 5: The greater the ability of a believer to evaluate and improve the credibility and value of beliefs, the more often that believer will evaluate and improve beliefs that lack credibility or value.

Proposition 6: Believers who have the knowledge and ability to evaluate and improve beliefs are likely to derive expectations from beliefs that are credible and valuable and, as a consequence, are likely to make choices and take actions to produce circumstances that are consistent with their beliefs.

answers to many of these questions. Your goal is to develop an informed judgment based upon the arguments presented, the six criteria for judging them, and what you know and how you reason about the arguments *and* the criteria.

Evaluation of Credibility

To evaluate the credibility of this theory, consider the *coherence, validity,* and *verifiability* of its propositions and conclusions as they appear in Table 2.1.

Coherence

Assess coherence by asking if the reasons in Table 2.1 hold together or cohere to form an understandable argument for the circumstance in question. Begin by examining Propositions 1 through 3. Do they make a coherent argument for why people prefer beliefs that are credible *and* valuable? Proposition 1 claims that credible beliefs are attractive because they predict the outcomes of various choices and actions, and Proposition 2 claims that valuable beliefs are attractive because they produce expectations that suggest appropriate choices to make and actions to take in different situations. Proposition 3 concludes that when beliefs are credible and valuable, choices and actions will be effective because they produce outcomes that are consistent with expectations. Therefore, it is in a person's interest to hold only credible and valuable beliefs. Does this argument hold together logically? Are extraneous or irrelevant reasons given that tend to confuse its claims? Do you think it is coherent?

Next, consider the coherence of Propositions 4 through 6. They claim that believers who have the knowledge and capacity to adopt beliefs that are credible and valuable are more likely to hold those beliefs than believers lacking knowledge and ability. Proposition 4 claims that believers who are knowledgeable about the credibility and value of beliefs are likely to derive expectations for choices and actions from such beliefs and thus to produce results that are consistent with expectations. Proposition 5 claims that the greater the ability of believers to evaluate and improve their beliefs, the more often they will evaluate and improve beliefs that lack credibility or value. Proposition 6 concludes that believers who have this knowledge and ability are likely to base their choices and actions on credible and valuable beliefs and that, as a consequence, they will produce circumstances that are consistent with their expectations. The implication is that, as a result of these beliefs, these believers will be more successful in adjusting to their circumstances.

Is this argument coherent? Do the reasons cited in the propositions relate logically to the central claim that believers who are knowledgeable and skilled at improving their beliefs will be more successful in adjusting to their circumstances? Are any of the assertions irrelevant to this claim and hence confusing to the argument? What about the six propositions taken together—do they cohere? Does each proposition contribute to the explanation for why people who prefer to hold credible and valuable beliefs may also hold beliefs that are not credible or not valuable? Are any propositions irrelevant to this claim? Do any of them conflict with each other or with the claim? Finally, what do you conclude about the theory's coherence?

Validity

To assess the validity of the theory, recall again that the six propositions offer two explanations: (a) People want to hold credible and valuable beliefs because they aid adjustment, and (b) they will hold these types of beliefs to the extent that they have the knowledge and ability to improve beliefs. Propositions 1 through 3 identify the reasons that credible and valuable beliefs are useful in adjusting to circumstances, and Propositions 4 through 6 identify the reasons that some people are more likely to hold credible and valuable beliefs than other people.

This is the structure of the theory. The conclusion in Proposition 3 follows from the reasons in Propositions 1 and 2 in that it depends upon them for truth support. You can test this by assuming Propositions 1 and 2 are true and then attempting to conclude that Proposition 3 is likely to be true as a consequence: in other words, by attempting to *infer* Proposition 3 from the premises in Propositions 1 and 2. If you can do this, the argument is probably valid.

Now do the same for the following in Propositions 4 through 6, which depend upon the argument in Propositions 1 through 3. Note the following relationships among these two sets of propositions:

1. If Propositions 1 and 2 are true, then Proposition 3 is likely to be true.

2. If Propositions 3, 4, and 5 are true, then Proposition 6 is likely to be true.

3. Therefore, if Propositions 1 through 5 are true, then Proposition 6 is likely to be true.

You can also test the validity of this reasoning by assuming that one or more of the propositions are false and noting if the truth of the conclusion changes as a result. For example, does assuming that Proposition 1 or 2 is false alter the truth value of Proposition 3, and does assuming that Propositions 1 through 5 are false alter the truth value of Proposition 6? Do these tests help you determine the validity of the theory?

Verifiability

The last credibility test is verification. It determines whether the propositions and conclusions of the theory are consistent with the circumstances they explain. If you cannot conduct this test, the theory's truth value cannot be determined. Its propositions may be coherent and conclusions valid, but the theory may nonetheless be false. Some theories are like this. They are coherent and valid, but they are not verifiable. Hence, they may be false.

To verify a theory, see if its propositions and conclusions correspond with the circumstances predicted or described. If they do, the theory is supported. Verifying the theory of credible and valuable beliefs requires test results of some sort to confirm or refute the claims of its six propositions. Given that Proposition 3 is inferred from Propositions 1 and 2, and Proposition 6 is inferred from

TABLE 2.2

Results of Hypothetical Test of Theory of
Credible and Valuable Beliefs

Matches Between Expectations and Accomplishments on Test Circumstance	Individuals With Knowledge and Ability About the Credible and Valuable Beliefs for a Test Circumstance (n = 100)	Individuals Without Knowledge and Ability About the Credible and Valuable Beliefs for a Test Circumstance (n = 100)
No. of individuals with matches	90	10
No. of individuals without matches	10	90

Propositions 1 through 5, a couple of approaches are possible. You can test all six propositions, or you can test the conclusions in Propositions 3 and 6. If you test the conclusions, you will be testing the entire theory because the conclusions are deduced from or implied by the other propositions. For example, testing Proposition 3 verifies the argument in Propositions 1 through 3, and testing Proposition 6 verifies the argument in Propositions 1 through 6.

Because we want to verify the entire theory, the latter option makes more sense. It also involves fewer tests. One possible approach to verification would be to gather data on different types of believers who were free to choose among the four types of beliefs to solve a test problem: credible and valuable beliefs, credible and worthless beliefs, suspicious but valuable beliefs, and suspicious and worthless beliefs. These believers could be divided into two groups: one group with knowledge and skills to evaluate the credibility and value various beliefs and the other group without that knowledge and ability. Next, the believers would receive a test problem to solve that would require setting expectations, making choices, and taking actions to produce results that were consistent with test beliefs. The prediction of the theory of credible and valuable beliefs would be that believers with the knowledge and ability would be more successful at this task than believers lacking knowledge and ability.

The results might look like those in Table 2.2, which show that 90% of the knowledgeable and capable believers produced results that matched their predictions, whereas only 10% of the ignorant and incapable believers produced accurate predictions. These results would support the theory, although they would not prove its truth. No verification test can do that. Tests only verify or falsify claims or predictions. Do you have any suggestions for other ways to verify this theory?

Evaluation of Worth

Knowing that a new theory is credible is necessary but not sufficient for deciding whether to adopt and use it. You also want to know if the theory improves your adjustments to various circumstances in life. You want to know if it offers a *valuable explanation* for those circumstances. There are three ways to evaluate a theory's value. The *significance* test determines the extent to which the theory reduces the discrepancy between understanding all the unusual circumstances of a situation and understanding little or nothing about them. The *scope* test evaluates the extent to which the theory explains other types of unusual circumstances. And the *utility* test determines the extent to which the theory guides practical adjustments to the misunderstood circumstance.

Significance

To fully understand the concept of significance, try to envision the conceptual distance separating the goal state of fully understanding an unusual circumstance from the actual state of not understanding the circumstance at all. With this image in mind, assume that you have discovered reasons that fully account for the discrepancy, making the actual state equal the goal state. Now you completely understand the unusual circumstance. Would you judge this explanation to be significant? I would, because your theory leaves nothing unexplained.

To illustrate with an example, consider the case of a person searching for a cure for her cancer. The actual state of understanding for this person is that she has a life-threatening disease but does not know what to do about it. Her goal state is to know how to completely rid herself of malignancy. This person would probably judge any theory that produces this result as significant. Unfortunately, there aren't any such theories. Different theories offer different solutions. One theory prescribes surgery, another recommends radiation therapy, and a third advocates chemotherapy. At different periods during her bout with the disease, this person adopted and used all three theories. When she believed in the surgery theory, she had a portion of the cancer removed. When she believed in radiation theory, another portion was eliminated. Then when she believed in the chemotherapy theory, the remaining cancer was eliminated. In combination, the three theories were significant because they fully eliminated the distance between not knowing what would eliminate cancer and knowing what would do it. Judged separately, however, none of the theories was significant.

This is the concept of significance. A theory is significant if it can eliminate the difference between what you want to know and what you know. Accordingly, the theory of credible and valuable beliefs is significant if it fully eliminates the difference between not knowing why people hold different types of beliefs and

TABLE 2.3

Typology of Credible and Valuable Beliefs

	Valuable Beliefs	*Useless Beliefs*
Credible Beliefs	Cell 1 Credible and Valuable Beliefs	Cell 2 Credible but Worthless Beliefs
Suspect Beliefs	Cell 3 Valuable but Suspect Beliefs	Cell 4 Suspect and Worthless Beliefs

knowing why some people hold only credible and valuable beliefs. Can the theory explain all this?

Table 2.3 classifies the four types of beliefs discussed in this chapter. Cell 1 represents beliefs that are credible and valuable, Cell 2 represents beliefs that are credible but not valuable, Cell 3 represents beliefs that are valuable but not credible, and Cell 4 represents beliefs that are neither credible nor valuable. Let us assume for this demonstration that the fourfold classification defines the universe of relevant beliefs about this problem. This will allow us to ask how much of this universe the theory of credible and valuable beliefs can explain.

The argument in Propositions 1 through 3 explains why people hold Cell 1 beliefs: because these beliefs help people adjust to various circumstances. If the theory were limited to these propositions, its conceptual significance would be 25% because it would account only for beliefs in one of the four cells. But the theory does more. Propositions 4 through 6 explain why people hold beliefs in Cells 2 through 4. These people hold suspect and worthless beliefs because they lack the knowledge and ability to evaluate and improve them. These propositions increase the theory's significance to 100% by expanding its explanation to include all four types.

Viewed this way, significance can be defined as a ratio of the explained to unexplained circumstances. Hence, the higher the proportion of explained to unexplained circumstances, the more significant the explanation is. If nothing is left unexplained, the theory is significant, but if much is left unexplained, it is not. Can you think of other ways to use this concept to test this theory's significance?

Scope

The second test of worth evaluates the extent to which a new theory explains other misunderstood circumstances. In general, comprehensive theories are more valuable than special theories because they explain more unusual circumstances. A comprehensive theory about the weather, for example, is more valuable than a special theory that predicts only rain. If your job were reporting weather, you would choose the theory that predicted everything—rain, snow, sleet, hail, thunderstorms, hurricanes, tornadoes, and everything else that constitutes substantial change in weather. Then you would be able to spend less time theorizing about the unknown and more time announcing predictions and giving advice.

Occasionally the term *general* describes this characteristic of theories. This should not be confused with the usage that implies a theory is useless because its prescriptions or predictions are too vague or general to be of any consequence. A *general* theory has a greater scope of applications than other theories. When Einstein labeled his second theory of relativity a general theory, he didn't mean it was less useful. On the contrary, he meant it was more useful because it explained a greater range of unknown circumstances in nature.

Applying the scope test to the theory of credible and valuable beliefs could focus on the *different types* of discrepancy problems that it explains. This would reveal that it covers three types of problems: (a) problems of not knowing *what causes* a circumstance (empirical problems), (b) problems of not knowing *how to judge* a circumstance (moral problems), and (c) problems of not knowing *how to act* on a circumstance (policy problems). It accomplishes this through constructive theorizing. You will see these applications in Chapters 3 through 5.

Utility

The utility test asks what difference it makes for someone to have knowledge offered by the new theory. It asks if holding the theory is useful in guiding decisions, actions, or adjustments during those pursuits that are worth engaging in. Again, the weather can illustrate. At one time, weather theories could predict only that rain might follow clouds. This was of limited use because no one wanted to carry umbrellas every day it was cloudy. These theories were credible, perhaps, but not but very valuable. Today, weather theories are more valuable because they predict where it will rain, when it will rain, how much it will rain, and how long the rain will last. Consequently, we depend on their forecasts to plan what to wear every day, what to do on a weekend, or where to go on a vacation. Now they affect many of our pursuits and adjustments.

Applied to the theory of credible and valuable beliefs, the utility test asks what difference it makes for people to know how to improve the credibility and value of their beliefs. The answer, according to the theory, is that having this knowledge and ability produces beliefs that can guide believers in what to expect from various choices and actions.

Believers who have the knowledge and ability to evaluate and improve beliefs are likely to derive expectations from beliefs that are credible and valuable and, as a consequence, are likely to make choices and take action to produce circumstances that are consistent with their beliefs (Proposition 6).

Given this benefit of knowing about credible and valuable beliefs, informed believers might react as follows:

> *Prediction 1:* Believers who do not get what they need and want because they hold suspect and useless beliefs are likely to want to learn how to improve or replace those beliefs.

> *Prediction 2:* Believers can improve the credibility and value of their beliefs by theorizing constructively to (a) identify discrepancies between beliefs and circumstances, (b) find reasons and construct explanations to eliminate those discrepancies, (c) evaluate the credibility and value of their new beliefs, and (d) adjust other beliefs on the basis of the understanding provided by their new beliefs.

> *Prediction 3:* Therefore, believers who do not get what they need and want because they hold suspect and worthless beliefs will strive to improve those beliefs if they have the opportunity to learn the skills of constructive theorizing.

In other words, this theory is useful if believers who adopt it react to the knowledge it provides by learning to use constructive theorizing to improve the credibility and value of their beliefs. Can you think of other ways the theory is useful?

STEP 4: ADJUST BELIEFS

Let us assume that this evaluation of the theory of credible and valuable beliefs has convinced you that it is worth adopting. This leads to the final step of constructive theorizing, which adjusts existing beliefs that may be inconsistent with this theory. If you identify any inconsistencies with other beliefs, you can theorize again by repeating the four-step process to resolve them. This will allow you to accommodate the new theory in a way that is consistent with other beliefs you hold about knowing what to believe. Of course, if you discover that none of your existing beliefs are inconsistent with this theory, you can move forward to consider the constructive theorizing demonstrated in Chapters 3 through 5. Perhaps the theories constructed in these chapters will provoke you to theorizing and then revising existing beliefs about how things work.

WHAT'S NEXT

This chapter set out to explain the contradiction between the claim that everyone prefers credible and valuable beliefs and the fact that many people hold beliefs that are not credible and not valuable. The chapter resolved this contradiction with four-step theorizing. The result was a theory of credible and valuable beliefs that explained why people who want to hold credible and valuable beliefs may hold beliefs that are neither credible nor valuable. These people hold suspect and worthless beliefs because (a) they lack information about which of their beliefs are suspicious or worthless and (b) they lack the ability to improve the credibility or valuable of those beliefs. Hence, they are stuck with inadequate beliefs.

The chapter also demonstrated how you could use six criteria to judge a theory's credibility and worth. You can evaluate *credibility* by examining the *coherence* of the reasons composing the theory, the *validity* of the conclusions implied by those reasons, and the *verifiability* or match between the theory's prediction and the circumstances it explains. You can evaluate a theory's *worth* by examining its significance, scope, and utility. A theory's *significance* reflects how much of the problem it can explain. Its *scope* reflects how many different problems it can explain. A theory's *utility* reflects how useful it is in guiding expectations, choices, and actions about practical situations.

Chapter 1 introduced you to a rationale for this thinking strategy called constructive theorizing, and Chapter 2 introduced a theory to justify it called the theory of credible and valuable beliefs. The next three chapters will use this strategy to improve ideological beliefs that claim to have final answers for why some people persistently suffer from unusual difficult circumstances in this country. Clearly, this is a challenging undertaking. Nevertheless, the approach to theorizing is the same. It solves each problem a step at a time.

Empirical Theorizing About Facts

This chapter employs empirical theorizing to answer the question "How do things work for people in need?" The result of this line of inquiry will be an empirical theory that explains how needy people adjust to their difficult circumstances in life. Chapter 4 employs moral theorizing to answer the question "How should things work for people in need?" It will produce a moral theory to judge the acceptability of those adjustments. And Chapter 5 employs policy theorizing to answer the question "What should be done for people in need?" It will produce a policy theory prescribing actions to ameliorate those adjustments.

We will begin this chapter's application of constructive theorizing with background information on beliefs about hardship and the empirical theories explaining how things work for the people experiencing it. The first two sections describe existing beliefs and theories that claim to account for why some people persistently fail to live a decent life in this country. The third section identifies inconsistencies in these explanations. This information will direct our theorizing as we attempt to understand inconsistent explanations about how things work.

BELIEFS ABOUT HARDSHIP

Although the reasons for hardship are often in dispute, its indicators are not. Some studies show, for example, that the people most likely to suffer from economic difficulty are women, members of minority groups, and people who are disabled. The data indicate that females earn 65% of male income, African Americans and Hispanics earn 58% of what whites earn, and the employment rate of people with mental or physical disabilities is at 33% (Shapiro, 1993, pp. 27-28; Wright, 1990, pp. 287-288). Moreover, people who experience unfavorable economic situations in the past are likely to suffer even more egregiously in the future, whereas people who experience favorable economic situations in the past are likely to maintain those advantages in the future. From this we might conclude that the country is becoming less egalitarian and, by implication, less fair. Hence the phrase "The rich are getting richer while the poor are getting poorer" may also apply (Carville, 1996, pp. 80-83).

Although social scientists and policy makers recognize that a sizable proportion of people suffer uncommonly difficult circumstances, they offer different and often contradictory explanations about the causes, their acceptability, and what to do about them (see Katz, 1986, 1989). The explanations that we will consider in this chapter and in Chapters 4 and 5 are reflected in beliefs about hardship derived from liberalism, conservatism, welfarism, and libertarianism.

Liberal ideology claims that people who experience economic hardship are not responsible for their plight because there is little they can do to change the circumstances that cause it. John Kenneth Galbraith took this view in *The Good Society: The Humane Agenda* (1996). He argued that restructuring institutions to equalize economic opportunity will ameliorate the economic disadvantages that some people experience. Conservative ideology, on the other hand, claims that people suffer economic hardship because they refuse to take responsibility for their own lives. Rather than solving their problems, they look to others for assistance during difficult times. Lawrence Mead, who made this point in *Beyond Entitlement: The Social Obligations of Citizenship* (1986), argued that it is wrong for people in need to seek assistance when they can do more for themselves. Therefore, government should force them to help themselves.

Welfare ideology claims that there will always be people incapable of caring for themselves and that society should protect them. Robert E. Goodin (1985), for example, asserted that the good society is responsible for securing the welfare of all members, which includes protecting the most vulnerable from unreasonable suffering. Finally, libertarian ideology claims that people in need fail to adjust adequately to their circumstances because they lack the effort, talent, and ability to get ahead in life. Richard Herrnstein and Charles Murray made this argument in *The Bell Curve: Intelligence and Class Structure in American Life* (1994) because they felt that winners would always be rewarded more than losers in society's inexorable evolution toward a meritocracy.

These ideologies are inconsistent with each other and with the experience of how things work for people in need. Consider their inconsistent claims about the causes and amelioration of hardship. Liberals argue that unequal social and economic circumstances cause some people to suffer more than others. Therefore, the collective should intervene to redress conditions of unfairness. Conservatives believe that people who suffer are the cause of their difficulties. Therefore, society should encourage them to solve their own problems. Welfarists believe that some people are incapable of taking care of themselves and hence are not responsible for the suffering they experience. Therefore, society should protect them. Libertarians believe that natural differences among individuals determine who succeeds and who fails in life. Consequently, there are always winners and losers, and nothing can change that.

THEORIES OF ADJUSTMENT

The empirical theories supporting these beliefs about how things work for people in need are also varied and somewhat contradictory. The relationships between behavioral theory, conservatism, and libertarianism are good examples. Behavioral theory explains how things work by postulating a functional relationship between behavior and a reinforcement contingency. It supports the conservative belief about needy people by claiming that a culture of poverty develops when environments reinforce maladaptive rather than adaptive behaviors. The result is a class of people who do not do enough to help themselves. The theory also supports the libertarian belief that sociocultural change reinforces some behaviors and punishes others to determine the adaptive responses of winners and losers in society. The result is a natural separation of people who have the innate capacity to adjust (the non-needy) from people who lack that capacity (the needy).

Now contrast the empirical theories that support the liberal and welfarist beliefs about the needy. According to autonomy theory, equal respect for the right to self-determination occurs when social institutions give all people control over their lives. It supports the liberal belief that social and economic circumstances affect personal autonomy and that when individuals in society fail to thrive on their own, their failure is due to these external social and political circumstances. The third theory for explaining how things work is rational choice theory. It claims that a rational calculus can identify the optimal adjustment for every member of society, regardless of physical, social, or economic circumstances. When applied to problems of the needy, it offers the prospect of preventing hardship by giving welfarists the means of protecting all of the most vulnerable in society from uncontrollable hardship.

We will use constructive theorizing to discover why these theories about how things work are inconsistent with each other and with the experience of adjustment. The four steps of constructive theorizing will direct this line of inquiry. Step 1 will define the discrepancy between the circumstances of adjustment and the theories of adjustment. Step 2 will find reasons to explain this discrepancy. Step 3 will evaluate the credibility and worth of the new explanation. Step 4 will adjust other beliefs that may be inconsistent with this new theory.

STEP 1: DEFINING THE DISCREPANCY

To begin this step, consider some of the most contradictory aspects of these theories about the adjustment process. Behavioral theory's claim that a controlling environment determines the life of a reactive adjuster appears to contradict the desire of humans to control their circumstances. Rational choice theory's claim that a rational calculus determines optimal adjustments appears to contradict the fact that we routinely depend on our experience rather than a calculation to decide how to adjust. And the claim that equal autonomy protection for all will ameliorate hardship contradicts the experience of people who act autonomously while experiencing persistent periods of hardship.

These contradictions notwithstanding, the three theories are very popular among academics and professionals who use them to explain, predict, and change various aspects of human behavior. Psychologists, educators, and social service personnel routinely apply principles from behavioral theory to develop intervention programs to improve individual adjustments (see, e.g., Sulzer-Azaroff, 1985). Economists and policy analysts use rational choice theory to predict individuals' choices in various social and economic situations.[1] And philosophers and political scientists use autonomy theory to critique and construct institutions to allow for greater expressions of freedom (see, e.g., Gaylin & Jennings, 1996; Held, 1991; Johnston, 1994; Raz, 1986).

These theories are so widely accepted and used that they cannot be dismissed simply because they may contradict experiences of adjustment like the ones just listed. Moreover, rejecting them because they fail a consistency test may eliminate them as a source of the problem we want to solve, but it does not explain the inconsistency. Given that this is our goal, we will begin here with problem solving that moves us from not knowing why a circumstance is inconsistent with a belief to knowing why it is. We will begin by trying to understand why the three theories of adjustment are inconsistent with each other.

Let us consider behavioral theory and rational choice theory first. Behavioral theory claims that all behavioral adjustments are a function of environmental consequences, and rational choice theory claims that all human adjustments are a function of rational choice. Are these claims really as contradictory as they appear? They are if you understand them to mean that human adjustment can be explained only by environmental consequences or by rational choices. However, if you understand the two claims to mean that they explain a different feature of the adjustment phenomenon, then perhaps not. Developing this line of reasoning might lead to the understanding, for example, that human rationality and environmental consequences work together to influence the adjustment process. Humans choose rationally by anticipating positive and negative consequences of a given adjustment, and those choices ultimately match consequences in the sense of being reinforced by them.

Can autonomy theory be analyzed in this manner too? It claims that adjustment is a function of autonomous actors constructing the circumstances defining who they are, what they expect in life, and what opportunities they deserve to reach their goals. Hence, people's capacity for autonomous action affects sociopolitical adjustments, not behavioral repertoires or a rational calculation (Taylor, 1989, p. 12). Is there any way to reconcile this claim in a manner similar to the reasoning that attempted to reconcile the claims of behavioral theory and rational choice theory?

STEP 2: FINDING REASONS FOR THE DISCREPANCY

One approach to explaining these inconsistencies is to examine the possibility that the three theories differ in the *scope* of their claims, the *focus* of their explanations, and the *components* of adjustment that they cover. On the dimension of scope, behavioral theory claims to account for the adjustment behavior of all organisms, human and nonhuman alike. Rational choice theory, by contrast, explains only choice making among humans, and autonomy theory explains only how choice functions in particular social and political environments. In this regard, behavioral theory is the most comprehensive because it explains how reinforcement contingencies influence the behavior of *any organism.* Rational choice theory is next in scope because it accounts for *any human's* use of rational calculations to identify relative gain from adjustment options. And autonomy theory is the least comprehensive of the three because it explains *an individual human's* use of freedom to choose from various social and political options.

Now let us examine how the theories differ in the *focus* of their claims. Behavioral theory explains how a person's *behavior* evolves toward a match with reinforcement contingencies in the environment. Rational choice theory explains how a person's *choices* tend to match various opportunities for gain based on a rational calculus. And autonomy theory explains how a person's *goals* correspond with various social and political opportunities for personal pursuits.

Clearly, these different explanations expand our understanding of adjustment. Behavioral theory advances our understanding of how behavior-environment interaction is influenced by reinforcement, punishment, and extinction. Behavioral adjustments improve for actors when the results of their choices are reinforcing. Rational choice theory advances our understanding of interaction between information seeking and the rational deliberation required to identify the optimal choice. Rational calculations about gain produce good choices. Autonomy theory also advances our understanding of how interaction between experience and expectations affects a person's prospects for achieving a valuable end in life. The person's preferences, which are based on those interactions, affect decisions to pursue one goal rather than another.

On both dimensions, the theories appear to be different rather than inconsistent *with each other.* They are not contradictory because (a) their explanations do not function at the same level of explanation (nonequivalence in scope) and (b) their accounts do not make claims about the same adjustment functions (nonequivalence in focus). They simply feature different aspects of the same phenomenon.

Still, these reasons do not explain why the three theories are inconsistent *with the circumstances of adjustment.* To understand why, let us examine (a) if the claims differ because they focus on different components of the adjustment process *and* (b) if this division of labor among the three theories explains why none of them is consistent with the experience of adjustment.

Let us turn our search for reasons to the four components of the adjustment process. When people adjust to change, they engage in four activities:

1. They set expectations for an adjustment based on their interests, needs, and abilities.

2. They search for information about the opportunities and obstacles to meeting those expectations.

3. They assess that information to make reasonable choices about the best opportunity under the circumstances.

4. They act on those choices to produce the results that they believe will be consistent with their expectations.

Which of these components do you think the three theories explain best? In my view, autonomy theory is best suited to explaining the *first* component, which focuses on a person's *purpose* for making an adjustment. Rational choice theory is best suited to explaining the *third* component, which focuses on the *thinking processes* that a rational person engages in to decide what to do. And the behavioral theory claim is most relevant to the *fourth* component, which focuses on how the frequencies of the person's *behaviors* adjust in the direction of the reinforcers available in the environment.

Again, the analysis suggests that the theories are not contradictory. But it also reveals something more, that none of the theories explains Component 2 on the information seeking that actors must do to learn about opportunities for improving adjustments. Clearly, this activity must be explained too.

Explanation 1

These reasons highlight the strengths and weaknesses of existing theories and, at the same time, suggest criteria for constructing a better theory. Accordingly, we should expect a new theory (a) to be consistent with explanations for how all organisms adjust to survive (to be as comprehensive as behavioral theory), (b) to differentiate human adjustment from nonhuman adjustment (to be as focused on humans as rational choice theory), (c) to differentiate one person's adjustments from another person's (to be as focused on individuals as autonomy theory), and (d) to account for all components of the adjustment process. If a new theory can accomplish all this, it will resolve inconsistencies associated with the three theories, and it will reduce or eliminate the discrepancy problem we defined in Step 1.

So let us begin this quest to develop a better explanation by identifying an explanatory mechanism for adjustment that satisfies the all four criteria. One that comes to mind is some version of *problem solving to meet a goal.* This is promising because it covers a full range of adaptable creatures, from the single-cell organism to the human being (Criterion 1). It even includes the adjustments of a tiny organism like the *E. coli* bacterium, as Max Perutz explained:

> Organisms are problem-solvers seeking better conditions [goal states]—even the lowest organism performs trial and error measurements with a distinct aim [goal]. This image brought to mind Howard Berg's striking film of chemotaxic bacteria. He showed how a bacterium's flagella motor makes it run and tumble randomly until the bacterium senses a gradient of nutrient. The bacterium then reduces the frequency of tumbling and lengthens the runs toward a greater concentration of nutrient. (quoted in Calvin, 1990, p. 31)

Although this description may appear too functionally distant from human problem solving to be of much use here, there are familiar elements to note, as neurobiologist William Calvin (1990) explained:

> [Most] philosophers looking through a magnifying glass at the food-finding path would have ascribed intelligence to the purposeful performance of the little bacterium. At such a marginal magnification, it would seem to "home in" on the morsel. But the bacterium has no brain: it's just a single cell with some inherited simple abilities such as swimming, tumbling, and sensing increasing yield. (p. 32)

Miller et al. (1960) used this conception of adjustment to postulate a self-regulating mechanism called the TOTE, which *can* describe human adjustment. They gave this mechanism three basic functions: (a) the identification of test variables that define preferred states, (b) the use of internal feedback that compares system conditions with those standards, and (c) a response to change in internal (system) and external (environmental) events. Then they applied it to explain all automatic adjustment processes and to account for the effects of reinforcement as postulated by behavioral theory:

> This is to say: (1) a reinforcing feedback must strengthen something, whereas feedback in a TOTE [test-operate-test-exit] is for the purpose of comparison and testing; (2) a reinforcing feedback is considered to be a stimulus (e.g., pellet of food), whereas feedback in a TOTE may be a stimulus, or information

(e.g., knowledge of results), or control (e.g., instructions); and (3) a reinforcing feedback is frequently considered to be valuable, or "drive reducing," to the organism, whereas feedback in a TOTE has no such value. (pp. 25-26)

Powers also used a TOTE-like mechanism to explain complex nervous system functions in humans. In *Behavior: The Control of Perception* (1973), he explained how this mechanism prompts self-regulatory activity that returns system functions to previous states. He argued that reference conditions in all nervous system functions are at zero baselines. However, when environmental inputs alter levels from that baseline, the system reacts by triggering regulatory reactions to return to baseline zero. According to Powers,

> The only reason for which way any higher organism acts is to counteract the effects of disturbances (constant or varying) on controlled quantities it senses. When the nature of these controlled quantities is known together with the corresponding reference conditions, variability all but disappears from behavior. (pp. 47-48)

The discrepancy-based conception of adjustment is also evident in John Dewey's (1933) description of human problem solving (see Chapter 1). Recall his claim that an inconsistency between circumstances and expectations provokes thinking to resolve the inconsistency. Dewey called this "reflective thinking . . . [which] involves (1) a state of doubt, hesitation, perplexity, mental difficulty, in which thinking originates, and (2) an act of searching, hunting, inquiring, to find material that will resolve the doubt, settle and dispose of the perplexity" (p. 12). Recall also Newell and Simon's (1972) mechanism that explains how all humans solve complex problems (see Chapter 1). It included three steps: (a) find the discrepancy between a goal state and current state, (b) find an operator to reduce the discrepancy, and (c) use the operator, and repeat the steps until the discrepancy is reduced.

What is encouraging about this explanation is that it appears to be consistent with behavioral theory in that it does not contradict it. It simply offers a different view of the process. According to behavioral theory, environments "shape" the behaviors of organisms through reinforcement from various environmental contingencies. And according to the discrepancy-based explanation, organisms solve problems of adjustment by searching for solutions to reduce differences between preferred and actual states. The behavioral explanation describes how environmental changes affect behavior, and the discrepancy-based explanation describes what organisms do to adjust to those changes.

This mechanism also appears to be consistent with rational choice theory because it does not contradict it either. According to the discrepancy explanation, adjustment *strategies* of humans and nonhumans differ due to the human capacity for cognitive problem solving. Hence, rational choice theory's identification of the rationally prudent choice for a given circumstance is simply a contributing factor in defining optimal adjustments for humans.

Explanation 2

Let us sum up what we have discovered in this effort to construct a better explanation for adjustment. We have learned from Explanation 1 that the discrepancy-based mechanism can probably meet the first criterion for developing a better theory because it claims that all organisms adapt by finding a means of reducing discrepancies between goal states and actual states. The mechanism can also meet the second criterion because, as indicated above, it is consistent with the cognitive problem solving that humans engage in to discover optimal adjustments to their situations.

Left unknown, of course, is whether the discrepancy-based explanation can also meet Criterion 3 on how persons individuate their adjustments and Criterion 4 on explaining all four components of the adjustment process. To find out about Criterion 3, let us consider how it functions when individuals engage in a series of adjustments over time. Imagine, for example, a cycle of adjustment, readjustment, and circumstantial change that accumulates favorable or unfavorable experiences over time. Next, envision some end point for that process and how it must reflect a changed person and a changed situation, as indicated by those accumulations. Is this not what autonomy theorists describe when they talk about individuals acting on their circumstances to create their lives? If it is, then this description is at least consistent with that theory in that it corresponds with the same phenomena associated with an individuating adjustment. It shows how repeated cycles of adjustment create new experiences and new circumstances and how these in turn create new emotional, cognitive, and behavioral experiences.

Now let us turn to Criterion 4, which requires our new theory to fully account for the complete process of adjustment. One way to check if it can meet this criterion is to compare the steps of discrepancy-based problem solving with the four adjustment components in Table 3.1. The discrepancy reduction steps are as follows. First, an adjuster experiences a discrepancy condition and sets an expectation to reduce it. Next, the adjuster considers opportunities (options) for meeting that expectation and makes the best choice available. Third, the adjuster acts to alter the circumstance in the direction of his or her expectation. Fourth, the adjuster compares an altered situation (results) with his or her expectation to determine if he or she reduced the discrepancy and solved the problem.

Compare these steps with those in Table 3.1 to see if they correlate with the emotional, cognitive, and behavioral experiences associated with adjustment. Here is one way to interpret the sequence. When people encounter a circumstance is inconsistent with their expectations for that situation, they react *emo-*

TABLE 3.1

The Four Components of Adjustment

When people adjust to a change in their circumstances, they engage in four activities:

1. They set expectations for those adjustments based on their interests, needs, and abilities.

2. They search for information about opportunities and obstacles that may be important to meeting those expectations.

3. They assess that information to make a reasonable choice about which opportunity is the best to pursue under the circumstances.

4. They act on that choice to produce the results that they believe will be consistent with their expectations.

---

tionally because they want to know if the unexpected event will affect their pursuits. This desire to know engages them *cognitively* as they seek information to find out what to do, if anything. This second component, in turn, provokes them to *act* on the circumstance according to their choice, the third component of the process. When they learn about the result, they examine it to determine if it is consistent with their expectations, the fourth component of the process. If it is, they are *satisfied* (emotionally) and no longer *feel a need* to adjust.

According to this interpretation, the discrepancy condition motivates actors to alter their expectations, choices, actions, and results in a chain of actions and reactions. Actors change their expectation in reaction to the discrepancy condition and then shift their attention to those circumstances that are relevant to reducing or eliminating their problem. Then they search for a means of producing the needed change by considering their options and choosing the one that produces the greatest reduction at the lowest cost to their time and resources. Next, they act with the expectation that their results will equal the gain they need to reduce or eliminate the problem. In other words, this causal sequence comes down to these four functions. *Expectations* are a function of the discrepancy problem, *choices* are a function of opportunities for reducing discrepancies, *actions* are a function of choices to act on the opportunity, and *results* are a function of the changed circumstance caused by the action.

Compare this account with the one described in Table 3.1. Note that the *expectation* variable in the new explanation is reflected in Step 1 in the table. The *choice* variable is reflected in the activities described in Steps 2 and 3. And the *response* and *result* variables are reflected in the adjustment activities described in Step 4. Does this explanation satisfy Criterion 4 of covering all four components of the adjustment process?

If it does, then perhaps we can also ask if this new explanation tells us anything we do not already know about the process described in Table 3.1. Can it explain, for example, what constitutes an *optimal* adjustment? Does it describe how a person's expectations, choices, actions, and results interact to produce the best outcome possible under the circumstances? To see if it does, read the following statements describing how the optimality states of people's expectations, choices, and actions will affect the optimality of their adjustment outcome. According to this reasoning, an optimal adjustment occurs when people's expectations, choices, and actions are optimal (as favorable as possible under the circumstances). Under these circumstances, people have done the best they can with their resources and their situation. They have adjusted optimally

1. When they set expectations that are optimal (just right) given their experience, eliminating similar discrepancy conditions

2. When they choose the most favorable opportunity (greatest gain at the lowest cost) for reducing the discrepancy

3. When they act efficiently while engaging the opportunity to reduce the discrepancy (a minimum of feedback seeking about what to do or how to do it)

4. When they produce the greatest gain possible toward reducing the discrepancy condition defining their adjustment problem

The following propositions formalize this new explanation. Taken together, they accomplish two goals. First, they cover all four components of adjustment described in Table 3.1. Hence, they meet Criterion 4 for developing a better theory. Second, they offer new knowledge by explaining the circumstances leading to an optimal adjustment:

1. *The Expectation Proposition*: The closer to optimal the past gain toward goal attainment (in a previous situation) and the smaller the discrepancy between the actual state and the goal state (in the present situation), the closer to optimal the expectation for gain (to reduce the discrepancy).

2. *The Choice Proposition*: The closer to optimal the past gain toward goal attainment and the more salient the differences between options, the closer to optimal the choice.

3. *The Response Proposition*: The closer to optimal the past gain, expectations, and choices, the closer to optimal the distribution of responses between task completion to meet the goal and feedback about goal state-actual state discrepancies, options, task performance, and gain.

4. *The Gain Proposition*: The closer to optimal the past gain, expectations, choices, and responses, the closer to maximum the gain toward goal attainment.

STEP 3: EVALUATING THE THEORY

Now it is time to evaluate the credibility and worth of this new theory. We will begin by asking if it offers an accurate explanation for how all persons adjust to unusual circumstances in life.

Is the Theory Credible?

To answer the credibility question, consider how judgments about the theory's coherence, validity, and verifiability might affect your confidence in its explanation. The *coherence* question asks if the explanation makes sense. The *validity* question asks if the conclusion implied by the theory follows logically from the theory's propositions. And the *verifiability* question asks if the theory is consistent with the actual circumstances of adjustment. Answers to these questions will help you decide if the theory is sufficiently credible to use when explaining why some people experience unfortunate adjustment outcomes in life.

Coherence

To judge the theory's coherence, ask if the reasons and explanations developed in this chapter made any sense to you. Did they provide coherent accounts for why autonomy theory, behavioral theory, and rational choice theory are inconsistent with each other and with the experiences of adjustment? Consider the reasons first. Did they offer a sensible account for why the three theories are inconsistent? Do you agree that the three theories differ primarily in scope (Reason 1), in focus (Reason 2), and on the adjustment component they cover (Reason 3)?

Next, consider the reasoning in the two explanations. Explanation 1 claimed that both humans and nonhumans solve problems by removing obstacles in the way of their goals. It claimed that humans adjust differently from nonhumans by solving problems cognitively rather than by trial and error. Explanation 2 claimed that individuals differ in their adjustments because they employ different means to reach different ends in life.

Do these explanations make sense? Are they relevant to knowing why the three theories fail to account for the entire process of adjustment? Remember that your answer to this question does not reflect a belief that the new theory is better than the other theories. It only reflects your assessment of its coherence with respect to the question. Last, ask if the four propositions of the theory are coherent. Do they make sense? Can you follow the reasoning that begins with Proposition 1 and ends with Proposition 4? If you can, the theory is probably coherent.

Validity

To assess validity, examine each proposition to determine if the last one follows logically from those preceding it. Or conversely, ask if the first three propositions imply the conclusion that optimal adjustment maximizes gain. Can you infer Proposition 4 from Propositions 1 through 3? To help in this analysis, I have substituted symbols for the variables in each proposition to reveal their arithmetic relationships. For example, Proposition 1 claims that the optimality of past gain, OPG, interacts with the amount of the discrepancy condition already reduced, A, to yield the optimality of the expectation, OE. Rewriting with symbols yields $OPG \times A = OE$. This means that the optimality of the past gain interacts with (is multiplied by) the magnitude of the discrepancy to yield (equal) the optimality of the expectation.

Doing the same for Proposition 2 shows that the optimality of the past gain, OPG, interacts with the salience of options (1 divided by the total number of options), SD, to yield the optimality of the choice, OC. This reformulation is $OPG \times SD = OC$. Similarly, Proposition 3 states that optimality of the past gain, OPG, the optimality of the expectation, OE, and the optimality of the choice, OC, interact to yield the optimality of the response, OR. This reformulation is $OPG \times OE \times OC = OR$.

For Proposition 4, the optimality of past gain, OPG, interacts with the optimality of the expectation for gain, OE, which interacts with the optimality of choice to produce that gain, OC, which interacts with the optimality of the responses, OR, to yield the maximum gain possible. This reformulation is $OPG \times OE \times OC \times OR = $ Maximum Gain.

The conclusion inferred from these propositions is that when each optimality factor is 1 (100% of optimal), then gain toward the discrepancy reduction is maximum. This implies as well that when any of the optimality factors is less than 1, the probability of maximum gain is less than 1. These conclusions follow logically from the propositions. To the question "When does optimal adjustment maximize gain?" the theory concludes, "When past gain, expectations, choices, and responses to the discrepancy condition are optimal."

Let us use these reformulated propositions to determine if the conclusions given below follow logically from the four propositions. Do this by substituting the value of 1 for each of the optimality factors and seeing what happens. Does it make the probability of maximum gain 1? Now substitute the value of 0 for each of the optimality factors, and note how this reduces the probability of maximum gain to 0. Any reduction in one of these optimalities reduces gain. This can occur (a) when the person has no experience with the discrepancy condition, $OPG = 0$; (b) when there is no discrepancy problem, $A = 0$; or (c) when there are no opportunities for producing gain and no salient differences among circumstances for making a choice, SD = 0.

1. *Expectation Proposition*: OPG × A = OE

2. *Choice Proposition*: OPG × SD = OC

3. *Response Proposition*: OPG × OE × OC = OR

4. *Gain Proposition*: OPG × OE × OC × OR = probability of maximum gain

5. *Conclusions*: Therefore:

▶ If OPG, OE, OC, *and* OR = 1, then probability of maximum gain = 1.

▶ If OPG < 1, then probability of maximum gain < 1.

▶ If OE < 1, then probability of maximum gain < 1.

▶ If OC < 1, then probability of maximum gain < 1.

▶ If OR < 1, then probability of maximum gain < 1.

In summary, the five conclusions are valid if you can deduce them from the four propositions. This does not mean, of course, that they are true. Their veracity depends upon the truth values of the supporting propositions. If they are true, the conclusions are likely to be true as well.

Verifiability

The third credibility question asks about the verifiability of the theory's propositions. How can we test them? One way is to check the theory's consistency with other theories. Another is to check its consistency with existing knowledge about the circumstances of adjustment. The analyses presented in this chapter suggested that this new theory might be consistent with autonomy theory, behavioral theory, and rational choice theory. Is it possible that the theory is also consistent with other theories of human behavior and adjustment? What about a research review of the adjustment components to determine if they are consistent with the theory's claims (Mithaug, 1993, pp. 100-116)? Direct tests of the theory through experiment and through your own activities of daily adjustment could confirm or refute its claims. You might determine, for example, whether the theory's optimality factors explain your own problem solving to improve adjustment outcomes. You could also design studies like those conducted by Newell and Simon (see Chapter 1) that used computer simulations to measure variations in each factor during various adjustment episodes (Mithaug, 1993, pp. 129-139).

The theory's propositions also provide guidance for their verification. They specify conditions that promote optimal adjustments and maximum gain during various problem-solving episodes. The following description of these conditions identifies some of these test conditions:

1. *The Expectation Proposition*: The closer to optimal the past gain toward goal attainment and the smaller the discrepancy between the actual state and goal state, the closer to optimal the expectation for gain. (Mithaug, 1993, p. 59)

Experience in producing gain toward goal attainment increases the individual's capacity to judge what is possible under the circumstances (options). The size of the discrepancy affects the individual's judgments, too. For example, the smaller the discrepancy, the more likely the person will find a gain (solution) that will either eliminate the difference or maximize its reduction. Conversely, as discrepancies between goal states and actual states increase, the probability of finding completely effective solutions decreases. Large discrepancy reductions frequently require multiple solutions with varying reduction effects. This makes it difficult to identify the option that produces incremental gain toward goal attainment. (Mithaug, 1993, p. 58)

2. *The Choice Proposition*: The closer to optimal the past gain toward goal attainment and the more salient the differences between options, the closer to optimal the choice. (Mithaug, 1993, p. 59)

The choice proposition specifies conditions under which the individual chooses the operation that produces the greatest gain at the lowest cost. Again, there are two factors that influence optimal choosing. The first is experience or past gain toward the goal: the closer to optimal the past gain, the more likely the person will select the best operation to produce expected gain. The second factor is the difficulty of identifying important differences between options. The proposition states that the more salient the difference between options, then the more likely the individual will choose optimally. During less than ideal choice circumstances where differences are subtle and options are many, discriminations are difficult and time consuming (costly). They reduce the likelihood of choosing optimally. (Mithaug, 1993, pp. 58-59)

3. *The Response Proposition*: The closer to optimal the past gain, expectations, and choices, the closer to optimal the distribution of responses between task completion to meet the goal and feedback about goal state-actual state discrepancies, options, task performance, and gain. (Mithaug, 1993, p. 59)

The response proposition specifies the conditions under which the individual maximizes responses to produce gain and minimizes responses that seek feedback. . . . Improvements in any of these conditions [of past gain optimalities, expectation optimalities, or choice optimalities] indicate the regulator's greater experience and understanding of what causes what. This leads to more effective and efficient distribution of responses. The person spends less time and effort monitoring performance accuracy, goal state-actual state discrepancies, options, and results and more time and effort performing the operations necessary to produce gain toward goal attainment. (Mithaug, 1993, pp. 59-60)

4. *The Gain Proposition*: The closer to optimal the past gain, expectations, choices, and responses, the closer to maximum the gain toward goal attainment. (Mithaug, 1993, p. 59)

The gain proposition describes the effects of adjustment optimalities on gain toward the goal. The proposition states that as past gains, expectations, choices, and responses approach maximum optimalities, gain toward reducing the discrepancy between the actual state and goal state maximizes, too. The upper limit—maximum gain—occurs when (1) past gain equals expected gain, (2) expectations for gain equal the maximum possible from the options available, (3) choices produce the greatest gain at the lowest cost, and (4) resource allocations maximize responding to produce gain and minimize feedback seeking on goal states, choices, performances, and gains. . . .

In summary, self-regulation theory states that you maximize progress toward goals when (1) past gains match expectations, (2) present expectations are the maximum possible, (3) choices are the best possible, and (4) follow-through on choice is as effective and efficient as possible. Under these conditions, regulation is optimal, and return from the environment is maximal. (Mithaug, 1993, pp. 60-61)

Is the Theory Valuable?

Now let us examine the theory's worth. Does it offer a significant, comprehensive, and useful explanation for adjustment? The theory is *significant* if it offers an explanation that completely eliminates our ignorance about how people adjust to unusual circumstances in life. It is *comprehensive* if it accounts for a full range of adaptive experiences. The theory is *useful* if its explanations and predictions offer guidance for making judgments and taking actions with regard to those outcomes.

Significance

To assess the theory's significance, bear in mind its description of relationships between expectations, choices, behavior, and results. They account for the experience as well as the process and outcomes of adjustment. In this sense, the theory is more significant than theories focusing only on experiences, only on cognitive calculation, or only on behavior. Therefore, when autonomy theory, rational choice theory, and behavioral theory are the comparison standard, the new theory appears to be significant.

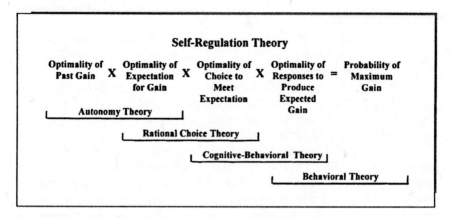

FIGURE 3.1. The Relationship Between Self-Regulation Theory and Other Adjustment Theories

The diagram in Figure 3.1 illustrates how self-regulation theory subsumes these explanations. Autonomy theory describes only the relation between experience (optimality of past gain) and aspirations (expectations for gain). Rational choice theory accounts only for relationships between expectations to maximize gain (optimality of expectation) and choices to minimize cost (optimality of choice). Cognitive-behavioral theory describes only relationships between choices (optimality of choice) and actions to implement choice (optimality of response).[2] And behavioral theory describes only the relationship between actions (optimality of responses) and reinforcements for those actions embedded in environmental circumstances (optimality of gain).

Scope

The scope test evaluates the range of the different adjustment outcomes that the theory can explain. To apply this test, ask if the new theory can account for such diverse adjustment problems as Herbert Simon's need to get his son to preschool *and* the motivation of Einstein-type scientists who construct theories about the universe. The theory covers both types of problem solving by showing how the discrepancy-based mechanism functions during problem solving to meet a goal. In the case of a routine discrepancy problem like that of Herbert Simon, the solution is known, and the challenge is finding a way of implementing it. But in the case of unusual problems, there is an uncertainty about what works, how it ought to work, or what should be done about it. Hence, repeated episodes of problem solving are necessary before an acceptable solution emerges.[3] Both cases are covered by the theory, mundane as well as unusual.

This theory also accounts for a range of emotions and experiences during adjustment. Think how you feel, for example, when a change in one optimality factor produces a change in others. At one end of the emotionality scale, you probably feel helpless when things do not go as you hoped, and at the other end of the scale you feel empowered when everything goes as expected. The theory explains by showing how interactions among the four optimality factors function to produce both an accumulation of negative experiences when things go wrong and an accumulation of positive experiences when things go right.

This occurs routinely during adjustment because any change in capacity or opportunity can affect prospects for a successful pursuit. If your *ability* to set expectations, choose opportunities, and act on those opportunities increases to improve your *prospects* for improving your circumstances, you will *feel empowered* to act. But if your ability decreases to negatively affect your prospects for improving your situation, you will *feel helpless* to act. This range of feelings and experiences is covered by the theory. It can account for the adjustments of people who are depressed because of their unfavorable adjustments to difficult circumstances *and* for the adjustments of people who are energized by what they have accomplished in life. This constitutes its range of explanatory applications.

Utility

The last worth test asks if the theory offers guidance for judging how things ought to work and for deciding what should be done about them. In the following chapters, you will see if this new knowledge helps answer these questions. For example, will knowing that people can adjust optimally to their circumstances and still experience poor prospects for success guide judgments about the fairness of those prospects? Also, will that knowledge guide decision making on what should be done about those circumstances? If so, then the knowledge provided by self-regulation theory about how adjustment works will have been useful.

STEP 4: ADJUSTING BELIEFS

The last step of constructive theorizing is to adjust other beliefs that may be inconsistent with this theory. To complete this step, we must proceed to the next chapters that identify beliefs that may be inconsistent with this theory. One of these is about the acceptability of those unfortunate adjustment outcomes and the other is about what should be done about them. Chapter 4 theorizes about inconsistent beliefs that judge the acceptability of unfortunate adjustment outcomes. Chapter 5 theorizes about inconsistent beliefs that prescribe what should be done about them, if anything. Both chapters demonstrate what happens when we attempt to adjust existing beliefs that are inconsistent with a newly adopted theory like this one.

NOTES

1. Becker (1986) claimed that it accounts for choices of "rich or poor persons, men or women, adults or children, brilliant or stupid persons, patients or therapists, businessmen or politicians, teachers or students" (p. 112).

2. This class of theories is similar to self-regulation theory. A review of them is in Mithaug (1993).

3. For additional explanations, see Chapters 7 and 8 in Mithaug (1993).

Moral Theorizing About Values

his chapter continues the quest to understand why the ideological beliefs about hardship introduced in the previous chapter are inconsistent with actual circumstances of need. In that chapter, we discovered why the theories supporting these ideologies—behavior theory, rational choice theory, and autonomy theory—are inconsistent with how adjustment works for all people. Left unexplained, however, was whether this new explanation is inconsistent with labeling the needy as victims, free riders, incompetents, and losers in order to help them. Does this method of judgment constitute fair treatment, and does it respect their rights to self-determination? Does it fairly reflect how things ought to work for people in need?

To find an answer to this moral question, we will follow the same four steps of constructive theorizing used to answer the empirical question of how things work for all people. We will begin by defining the problem as a difference between knowing and not knowing something. Here it is between knowing how the adjustment process works for everyone, as explained by self-regulation theory, and not knowing whether or why it is inconsistent with ideological labeling. Then we will search for reasons to explain and eliminate this difference. Next, we will evaluate the credibility and worth of the theory constructed in Step 2. We will conclude by adjusting existing beliefs that are inconsistent with our new moral theory.

STEP 1: DEFINING THE DISCREPANCY PROBLEM

To begin, let us examine the basis of ideological labeling. We know from Bernard Weiner's (1995) research on judgments of responsibility, for example, that ideological beliefs are based upon different perceptions about capacity and responsibility. The beliefs about need introduced in the previous chapter reflect these perceptions too. Two of them are based on the assumption that individuals are equal in their capacity to adjust to various circumstances in life, and two are based on

69

TABLE 4.1

Judgments About Adjustment Outcomes Based on
Individual Capacity and Responsibility

	Assumption 1 Individuals Are Not Responsible for Their Adjustment Outcomes	Assumption 2 Individuals Are Responsible for Their Adjustment Outcomes
Assumption 3 Individuals Are Equal in Their Capacity to Adjust	Cell 1 Compassion for "Victims" (Liberals)	Cell 2 Blame for "Free Riders" (Conservatives)
Assumption 4 Individuals Are Unequal in Their Capacity to Adjust	Cell 3 Pity for "Incompetents" (Welfarists)	Cell 4 Praise for "Winners" Sympathy for "Losers" (Libertarians)

NOTE: This analysis is based in part on the research and analyses presented by Weiner (1995).

the contrary assumption that people are unequal in capacity. The same goes for assumptions about responsibility. Two of the beliefs rest on the assumption that people are equally responsible for everything that happens to them, and two rest on the contrary assumption that people are not equally responsible.

On the equal capacity assumption, liberalism and conservatism share the view that all persons have roughly the same innate capacity to adjust to their circumstances, and on the unequal capacity assumption, welfarism and libertarianism share the opposite view that individuals have very different capacities to deal with their circumstances. On the unequal responsibility assumption, by contrast, liberalism and welfarism share the view that needy persons should be excused from responsibility for solving their problems, and on the equal responsibility assumption, conservatism and libertarianism share the view that people in need should be as responsible for solving their problems as people who are not needy.

Four Ideological Judgments of Need

These assumptions provide the basis for the four judgments about need. Table 4.1 illustrates, with Cell 1 representing the liberal belief, Cell 2 representing the conservative belief, Cell 3 representing the welfarist belief, and Cell 4 representing the libertarian belief. We will consider each in turn.

Equal Capacity and Unequal Responsibility (Cell 1)

Liberals believe many perfectly capable people who are needy cannot be held responsible for their adjustment outcomes because society distributes opportunities unequally. This denies them a fair chance to live the good life that everyone else enjoys. They are, as Cell 1 in the table indicates, victims of an unfair system and hence free of blame for the hardship they experience. John Kenneth Galbraith espoused this belief in *The Good Society* (1996), which described the conditions of opportunity that all members in society deserve:

> In the good society all of its citizens must have personal liberty, basic well-being, racial and ethnic equality, the opportunity for a rewarding life. Nothing, it must be recognized, so comprehensively denies the liberties of the individual as total absence of money. Or so impairs it as too little. (p. 4)

James Carville made a similar argument in *We're Right, They're Wrong* (1996), blaming society rather than the individual for unreasonable suffering:

> Wages have stagnated or declined in America for the past two decades. The folks at the top have been making out fine. But the bottom 80 percent of the American workforce hasn't seen a pay raise, when you factor in inflation, since the 1970s.
> The wealth and income in this country is becoming increasingly concentrated in the hands of fewer and fewer people. By the mid-1980s, we had the biggest gap between haves and have-nots in the entire industrialized world. (p. 77)

Equal Capacity and Equal Responsibility (Cell 2)

Compare this view with the conservative claim that assumes people are equally capable and responsible for their own circumstances in life. According to this view, all persons must do as much as possible to overcome their difficulties. If they don't, they are to blame, not society. Needy people usually experience persistent difficulties in life because of their wasteful ways, shortsightedness, and unwise decisions. The following examples express these beliefs about people on welfare:

- Don Boys, a former member of the Indiana House of Representative was quoted as saying, "Many Welfare Mamas are, as the old-timers used to say, very 'fleshy,' sucking on cigarettes, with booze and soft drinks in the fridge, feeding their faces with fudge as they watch the color TV" (quoted in Albelda, Folbre, and Center for Popular Economics, 1996, p. 16).

■ Senator Phil Gram, as paraphrased by columnist George F. Will, stated that "Welfare recipients are people 'in the wagon' who ought to get out and 'help the rest of us pull'" (quoted in Albelda et al., 1996, p. 26).

■ According to Mickey Kaus, "Both AFDC and Food Stamps flout the work ethic, offering support to able-bodied Americans whether they work or not—the only major components of our 'welfare state' that do this. Social Security's retirement benefits, in contrast, go only to workers" (quoted in Albelda et al., 1996, p. 28).

■ Governor Pete Wilson of California, who proposed a 9% cut in Aid to Families with Dependent Children, stated, "I am convinced they will be able to pay the rent, but they will have less for a six-pack of beer. I don't begrudge them a six-pack of beer, but it is not an urgent necessity" (quoted in Rank, 1994, p. 3).

■ A Massachusetts state senator described his state's welfare program for able-bodied adults as follows: "General Relief goes to people who are urinating on the floor in the bus station in Brockton and throwing up. They take that $338 and go to the nearest bar and spend it" (quoted in Rank, 1994, p. 3).

Unequal Capacity and Unequal Responsibility (Cell 3)

A third way to view hardship is to assume, as welfarists do, that people lacking the capacity to improve their situation should be protected. They are helplessly overcome by their circumstances and, as a consequence, are not responsible for their problems. Mickey Kaus expressed this view in *The End of Equality* (1992). He stated that there will always be people who are cognitively deficient and hence condemned to a life of marginal adjustment. He cited Richard Herrnstein's (1971) theory of innate deficiency as proof. In this famous 1971 *Atlantic Monthly* article, Harvard psychologist Richard Herrnstein used this possibility as the basis for the following disturbing syllogism:

1. If differences in mental abilities are inherited, and

2. If success requires those abilities, and

3. If earnings and prestige depend on success,

4. Then social standing (which reflects earnings and prestige) will be based to some extent on inherited differences among people. (p. 43)

Kaus (1992) wanted to protect these unfortunate persons from feelings of social inferiority that inevitably result when more gifted and talented people receive all the rewards in life. He called this the "Loser Problem:"

The Loser Problem is the possibility that, in any money hierarchy—even a flexible, impermanent, True Meritocratic money hierarchy—those on the bottom, the losers, will feel they somehow deserve to be on the bottom. The bottom, after all, is where some people will wind up. If they feel therefore inferior, that's likely to be bad for social equality. . . .

Indeed, in a True Meritocratic society, with its bouquet of opportunities to demonstrate specific talents, its lack of arbitrary barriers, its constant, continuing judgments about performance, people are likely to feel that the implicit decision rendered by their success in the marketplace is all the more valid. Here we come to a great nasty irony that inflames the Loser Problem, an irony that might be called the Fairness Trap: *The more the economy's implicit judgments are seen as being fair and based on true "merit" (and "equal opportunity"), the more the losers will tend to feel they deserve to lose, the easier it will be to equate economic success with individual worth, and the greater the threat to social equality.* (pp. 47-48)

Unequal Capacity and Equal Responsibility (Cell 4)

The fourth ideological belief is based on the assumption of unequal capacity and equal responsibility. It claims that although people in need are less capable than others in society, they nevertheless are fully (equally) responsible for dealing with their situation as best they can. That they persistently lose in the competition for gain is a fact of life in societies valuing achievement based on merit. William A. Henry expressed this view in his book *In Defense of Elitism* (1994). He argued that ignoring innate differences among individuals will erode the basis of cooperation and the standards used to judge merit. Already, he stated,

American society has lost the confidence and common ground to believe in standards and hierarchies. We have taken the legal notion that all men are created equal to its illogical extreme, seeking not just equality of justice in the courts but equality of outcomes in almost every field of endeavor. Indeed, we have become so wedded to this expectation that our courts may now accept inequality of outcomes as prima facie proof of willful bias. (p. 13)

Henry concluded that all people deserve to be rewarded for outcomes they are responsible for producing on their own:

In pursuit of egalitarianism, an ideal wrenched far beyond what the founding fathers took it to mean, we have willfully blinded ourselves to home truths those solons well understood, not least the simple fact that some people are better than others—smarter, harder working, more learned, more productive, harder to replace. (p. 14)

Charles Murray, coauthor of *The Bell Curve,* used the same reasoning in *Losing Ground: American Social Policy 1950-1980* (1984):

> Some people are better than others. They deserve more of society's rewards, of which money is only one small part. A principal function of social policy is to make sure they have the opportunity to reap those rewards. Government cannot identify the worthy, but it can protect a society in which the worthy can identify themselves. (p. 234)

Inconsistencies Among Ideological Judgments

Now perhaps you can see how different assumptions justify different labels for the needy. Assumptions supporting the liberal point of view, for example, justify the use of the *victim* label, which *excuses people in need from responsibility* for their hardship. Assumptions supporting the conservative point of view justify labeling the needy as *free riders* because *they do not act responsibly* to improve their circumstances. Assumptions supporting the welfarist position justify labeling the needy as *incompetent* because they are *incapable of acting responsibly* to help themselves. And assumptions supporting the libertarian point of view justify labeling the needy as *losers* because they *cannot compete successfully* for a favorable position in society.

If you examine Table 4.1 again, you will see this reasoning at work. The columns represent assumptions about responsibility, and the rows represent assumptions about capacity. By arguing from Cell 1, formed by Assumptions 1 and 3, liberals can show compassion by offering compensation for people who have been denied equal opportunities in life. Such people are victims of the unfair circumstances described by Galbraith in *The Good Society* (1996) and Carville in *We're Right, They're Wrong* (1996). By arguing from Cell 2, formed by Assumptions 2 and 3, conservatives can blame able-bodied people for seeking public assistance without first doing their part to help themselves. Here needy people are the free-rider targets of rebuke identified in William J. Bennett's *The De-Valuing of America: The Fight for Our Culture and Our Children* (1992) and in Lawrence M. Mead's *Beyond Entitlement: The Social Obligations of Citizenship* (1986).

Now consider the remaining two cells. By arguing from Cell 3, formed by Assumptions 1 and 4, welfarists can feel pity for incompetent people overwhelmed by circumstances beyond their control. Mickey Kaus expressed this sentiment in *End of Equality* (1992). Finally, by arguing from Cell 4, formed by Assumptions 2 and 4, libertarians can feel sympathy for society's losers who fail to secure a share of gain in the meritocratic competition necessary to construct a decent life in the free society. Henry expressed these sentiments in *In Defense of Elitism,* as did Murray in *Losing Ground* (1984).

Stripped to their theoretical bones, these familiar ideological arguments label needy people according to these four assumptions about their capacity and responsibility. What do you think of this belief system? Is it sufficiently comprehensive to cover all people who suffer unreasonable hardship in life? Does it constitute fair treatment for people who seek help? And is it consistent with the expectation that even the needy have a right to be respected when seeking assistance?

Before answering, think about how you might react if you were to suffer a significant setback in your prospects for getting what you needed and wanted in life. Would your unforeseen circumstance fit one of the need cells in Table 4.1? Would it qualify you for help as a victim, as a free rider, as an incompetent, or as a loser? Or would you expect a category of need unique to your situation? My guess is that you would insist on the latter. I know I would.

Putting yourself in the shoes of the needy clarifies the discrepancy problem we want to resolve. It reveals the troubling feature of any classification system that is inconsistent with actual circumstances of need or hardship. It raises the possibility that the judgments reflected in these labels are baseless and hence unfair. This in turn raises the equally troubling possibility that these judgments also offend, if not harm, the labeled person's sense of autonomy and freedom. This is the discrepancy between "how things actually work for people in need" and "how things ought to work for them" that we want to resolve. It suggests that how things work in defining a person's eligibility for help *may not be right*.

STEP 2: FINDING REASONS AND CONSTRUCTING EXPLANATIONS

Let us try to resolve this discrepancy problem by searching for reasons to explain three inconsistencies. The first is between this system of judgment and how adjustment actually works for all people as explained by self-regulation theory. The second is between these judgments and the expectation for fair treatment of all people, regardless of their circumstances of need. And the third is between these judgments and the expectation that all persons, including the needy, deserve to be respected as individuals who have the autonomy and freedom to fully participate in mainstream society on their terms.

Reasons for Inconsistency 1: The Circumstances of Adjustment

To resolve the first inconsistency, it is helpful to recall what we know from self-regulation theory about how adjustment works, namely that no one adjusts in the manner suggested by the assumptions in Table 4.1. People adjust in accordance with four optimality factors identified by self-regulation theory. They adjust according to their *experience* of producing gain toward a valuable end in their life, their *expectations* to change circumstances in that direction, their *choices* about opportunities for producing that change, and their *actions* on their choices. Moreover, needy and non-needy people alike adjust optimally when they have had an experience solving a similar adjustment problem, when they make an optimal choice given the alternatives, and when they take optimal action under the circumstances. In every situation and for every person, *experience* affects beliefs about *capacity,* which in turn affect judgments about *opportunities* to act effectively to produce change. All these factors combined affect *prospects* for reaching desirable ends in life.

Hence, this knowledge about adjustment can predict prospects for success as follows. If people lack experience in solving an adjustment problem, their prospects for success decline. If they lack the capacity (resources) to improve an unfavorable circumstance, their prospects for success decline. And if they do not have a favorable opportunity for using their resources to produce the change needed to reach their goals, their prospects for success decline. Any of these factors can reduce their prospects and affect their choices and decisions to act. Under some circumstances of need, people will judge their situation to be too risky to act on because the drain on their resources in making the attempt is too great given the promise of success. So their decision not to act in this situation is as optimal an adjustment as their decision to take action in another situation, according to self-regulation theory. What is optimal and what is not varies circumstantially for each person.

The point to underscore once again is that this is how all people adjust, not just how the very needy or the very wealthy adjust. Everyone weighs the costs and gains of altering a given situation at a given time. When costs outweigh prospects for success, people avoid an attempt. But when the promise of success outweighs the cost of the effort, they make the effort. This is how the factors identified by the theory influence decisions to act. It is how people take into account their *past experience* at producing gain, their *expectations* for producing gain with a change in circumstances, their *choices* to use their resources to produce that change, and their *actions* to produce the change. It is also how interactions among these factors affect adjustment optimalities, the level of gain experienced from that adjustment, and the judgment of success or failure of that effort.

This new theory tells us that knowing what is optimal requires accounts of *actual interactions* between people's capacity and opportunity rather than an *assumption* about their *capacity* and *responsibility*. When people's capacity is sufficient to engage an opportunity, their prospects for success will be sufficiently good to risk acting. On the other hand, when their capacity is inadequate for the occasion, taking action is too risky. In both situations, the basis for acting is the match between their capacity and opportunity. Changes in either factor may alter the decision to act by changing its prospects for success. Optimal adjustments are a function of these best estimates of the outcomes likely for a given capacity-opportunity interaction.

Given this understanding, it makes sense to judge people's outcomes according to their *particular* capacities and opportunities for getting what they need and want in life. The problem is that this is not the basis of the judgments in Table 4.1. The liberal judgment that all needy people are victims and deserve compassion assumes that they lack control of their circumstances. According to self-regulation theory, however, many people can be in need and also be optimal adjusters dealing as effectively as possible under the circumstances. Simply because they face difficulties in their lives does not mean they should be treated with *compassion* because their circumstances *are beyond their control.* It is as appropriate to afford them *respect* and *admiration* for dealing imaginatively and effectively with circumstances that are *very difficult to control.*

The conservative judgment that needy people should be blamed because they have not done enough to help themselves assumes that acting on your circumstances makes you more prudent in your decision making than not acting on them. Self-regulation theory offers a plausible alternative here also. A needy person may be adjusting optimally by deciding not to waste time, energy, and material resources attempting to improve a risky situation. In the same sense, an advantaged person may be adjusting optimally by deciding to invest additional time, energy, and material resources to improve an already favorable situation. Both decisions are optimal under these circumstances. Hence, there is no justification for blaming the first person and praising the second without additional information. Unfortunately, ideological assumptions supporting free-rider labels force this error in moral judgment.

The self-regulation explanation also contradicts the welfarist view that some needy people are so mentally, physically, and socially incompetent that they deserve society's pity. People with disabilities often get this label due to the public's perception that they are subnormal in every vital aspect of personhood. Again, understanding that people vary in their capacity and opportunity challenges this assumption about persistent incapacity. Even well-intentioned welfarists like Mickey Kaus worry about the damage to self-esteem resulting from persistent failure in life. Apparently, Kaus does not understand that being treated like a child who is incapable of controlling his or her life is likely to undermine anyone's self-respect. Again, self-regulation theory redirects attention to the importance of personal control over those capacity-opportunity interactions that affect prospects for reaching valuable ends in life.

The libertarian claim that people who do not get what they need and want in life are losers is not supported by self-regulation theory either. This claim overlooks the fact that variation in capacity and opportunity can produce cycles of gain and loss, leading to an acceleration of advantage on some occasions and an acceleration of disadvantage on others. These cycles work as follows. When people alter circumstances in a favorable direction during one episode, they improve their prospects for acting effectively in subsequent episodes because they require fewer resources to advance their projects. Moreover, if this pattern persists until they complete their projects, they end up with greater net capacity and more favorable opportunities, which further improve their prospects for success. The same occurs in reverse when they fail to change their circumstances in the direction of their goals. The expenditure of resources needed for the effort leaves them with less capacity to improve their situation on subsequent attempts. This, in turn, decreases their prospects for goal attainment. Moreover, each additional failure decreases their prospects further. The point is that neither cycle reflects a person's innate superiority or inferiority compared to other people, as libertarians claim. Instead, both cycles reflect the effect of an interaction between capacity and opportunity that yields a changed prospect for success.

To sum this up, self-regulation theory tells us that circumstances of adjustment vary more dramatically within and across individuals than ideological assumptions about fixed capacity and fixed responsibility can possibly cover or adequately reflect. Therefore, labels like *victim, free rider, incompetent,* and *loser* are irrelevant and perhaps inappropriate for most needy people because their circumstances fall outside these narrowly defined parameters justifying help.

Reasons for Inconsistency 2: The Principle of Fairness

This conclusion leads to a second set of questions that we must consider. If ideological labeling is inappropriate in many cases, is it appropriate and fair in any case? Are there any circumstances of need that can justify calling a person a victim, a free rider, an incompetent, or a loser? Is any labeling ever fair?

Table 4.2 presents possible answers to these questions. It describes versions of fairness that cover different *types of actors* and different *types of circumstances.* The columns of the table identify doctrines of fairness covering relationships between society and the individual (Column 1) and relationships among individuals (Column 2). The rows of the table identify doctrines of fairness covering access to the means (Row 1) and access to the ends (Row 2) of various adjustment pursuits.

The doctrines formed by the cells of the table correspond cell by cell to the four ideologies in Table 4.1. The columns of the table show, for example, that liberal and welfarist doctrines focus on fair relationships between society and the individual (Column 1) and that conservative and libertarian doctrines focus on fair relationships among individuals (Column 2). The rows of the table indicate

TABLE 4.2

Different Doctrines of Fairness

	Fairness in the Group	*Fairness Among Individuals*
Fairness in the Means Fairness in the distribution of rights and responsibilities	*Cell 1: Liberals* Fairness is equal protection from society through equalized opportunities for all members.	*Cell 2: Conservatives* Fairness is equal protection from others through equalized responsibility for persons.
Fairness in the Ends Fairness in the distribution of rewards and benefits	*Cell 3: Welfarists* Fairness is equal protection from society through equalized benefits based on group membership.	*Cell 4: Libertarians* Fairness is equal protection from others through rewards for individual pursuits based on merit.

that liberal and conservative doctrines focus on equality of access to the *means* of various self-determined pursuits (Row 1) and that the welfarist and libertarian doctrines focus on access to the benefits resulting from reaching the *ends* of those pursuits (Row 2).

Cell 1 fairness supports the liberal view that people in need should to be *protected equally* from an oppressive majority through societal restructuring to equalize opportunities. Cell 2 fairness supports the conservative view that individuals should be *protected equally* from each other through enforcement of full-responsibility rules. Cell 3 fairness supports the welfarist view that individuals should be *protected equally* from uncontrollable harm through the equalization of benefits due them as helpless members of society. Cell 4 fairness supports the libertarian view that individual pursuits should be *protected equally* by guarantees that all benefits from those pursuits will be distributed to individuals on the basis of merit.

Now compare these doctrines with assumptions about capacity and responsibility in Table 4.1. Cell 1 fairness justifies redressing the harm caused by victimization. Cell 2 fairness justifies the demand that needy free riders help themselves. Cell 3 fairness justifies protecting incompetent people who are helpless in dealing with their difficulties. And Cell 4 fairness justifies doing nothing to help the needy that will jeopardize rewarding deserving individuals for their accomplishments. Do you agree that these fairness doctrines justify labeling people in need? Or do you think that a proviso like the following is necessary to make the system more reasonable, if not more acceptable?

> To the extent that a needy person's circumstances match the assumptions of capacity and responsibility in Table 4.1, labeling individuals according to those criteria is appropriate because the doctrine of fairness in Table 4.2 justifies those labels.

Reasons for Inconsistency 3: Autonomy and Opportunity

Before answering, let us consider the last inconsistency, between ideological labeling and the expectation that every person's right to self-determination should be protected equally. The concern here is that the act of affixing a pejorative label on any person is dehumanizing in that it adversely affects the person's prospects for living a decent life in the community. This concern emanates perhaps from the suspicion that any time someone is called a victim, free rider, incompetent, or loser, that person will probably suffer greater marginalization in his or her pursuits than people who avoid stigmas. Indeed, history is replete with the use of pejorative labels by majorities to limit the opportunities of minorities.[1]

We want to know if this is happening here. If it is, then we have a truly troubling situation given that the four ideologies claim to advance the democratic ideals of liberty and equality for all. This possibility causes us to wonder how pejorative labeling like that in Table 4.1 can be good for any needy person's prospects for living the self-determined life. This is the question we want to answer. What possible reasons can be adduced to make this counterintuitive claim that labeling is a good thing to do to another person, regardless of his or her circumstances?

One way to reason out of this conundrum may be to claim that the goal of all four ideologies is to protect the long-term interest of everyone in society. Table 4.3 develops this reasoning by showing a plausible association between the ideologies and their specialized methods of maximizing freedom and autonomy for all people, including the needy. The columns of the table present two ways of maximizing freedom, and the rows present two ways of maximizing autonomy. Column 1 focuses on increasing *freedom from* constraint and column 2 focuses on increasing *freedom to* act.[2] Row 1 focuses on equalizing opportunity and responsibility, and Row 2 focuses on guaranteeing security and rewarding merit.

These doctrines of autonomy and freedom are supported by the four ideologies as follows. Liberals argue from Cell 1 that people's autonomy is maximized when they are *free from* obstacles to pursue their plans for a good life. Maximization occurs when all members in society have roughly the *same opportunities* to succeed. Conservatives argue from Cell 2 that people's autonomy is maximized

TABLE 4.3

Different Methods of Maximizing Autonomy and Freedom

	Maximize Negative Freedom	*Maximize Positive Freedom*
	Cell 1: Liberals	*Cell 2: Conservatives*
Maximize autonomy by equalizing opportunities and responsibilities	Maximize negative freedom by equalizing opportunity	Maximum positive freedom by equalizing responsibility
	Cell 3: Welfarists	*Cell 4: Libertarians*
Maximize autonomy by guaranteeing security and rewarding merit	Maximize negative freedom by guaranteeing security	Maximize positive freedom by rewarding merit

when they are *free to* pursue their own interests. This is maximized when all persons *take full responsibility* for their actions. Welfarists argue from Cell 3 that autonomy increases when people are *free from* the threat of unreasonable hardship in life. This is maximized when the collective guarantees *security* for all, including those who are most vulnerable. And libertarians argue from Cell 4 that autonomy is maximized when people are *free to* produce and keep what they earn through their self-determined pursuits in life. This is maximized when all members of society are rewarded on the basis of *individual merit.*

Does the promise of greater benefits for everyone in society offset the stigma of labeling a few in society? Here are some arguments claiming that it does. The liberal justification is that although being labeled a victim is unpleasant, the promise of equalized opportunity for all offsets this temporary discomfort. The conservative justification is that being called a free rider is intentionally unpleasant so that people will be discouraged from taking unfair advantage of their freedom. The welfarist justification is that labeling people as hopelessly helpless is necessary to identify who is truly needy and deserving of protection. The libertarian justification is that being a loser is an unavoidable consequence of failing to win in the competition of the most meritorious.

Explanations

Now we have three explanations for inconsistencies between how things work for people in need and how they ought to work for them. The first is that holders of ideological beliefs about the needy believe that labeling is justified by the assumptions about people's capacity and responsibility described in Table 4.1. The second is that ideologues believe that this system of labeling is fair for the reasons identified in Table 4.2. The third explanation is that they believe their labels are ultimately beneficial for all because the policies justified by these labels will lead to greater freedom and autonomy for all, as Table 4.3 reasons.

Are these explanations sufficient for us to adopt this system of judgment when trying to decide on the acceptability of circumstances adversely affecting people in need? Probably not, because we are still left with the knowledge that this system of judgment does not account for the many variations in adjustment that people in need experience in their lives. And *having this knowledge* undermines the status of this system's supporting doctrines of fairness and freedom. Knowing what we do about adjustment suggests that if this system is relevant at all, it is useful only in a very narrow sense because what remains unexplained is a wide band of circumstances of need that is irrelevant to and inconsistent with the assumptions about individual capacity and responsibility that justify ideological labeling.

The only option left, therefore, is to construct a better moral theory. We must find a way of judging circumstances of need based on fair relationships and equal prospects for success among all members of society, needy and non-needy alike. The solution we are looking for is a method of judgment that embraces Mark Robert Rank's (1994) standard for treating all people fairly, poor and nonpoor alike:

> The welfare recipient is not that different from you or me—no better, no worse. Nevertheless, we Americans often view welfare recipients as somehow different from the rest of us: they live in inner cities, they have too many children, they are irresponsible and don't work hard enough; in short, they get what they deserve. . . .
>
> *Our policy discussion should be based not upon how different the poor are from the rest of us but rather upon how much they have in common [with us]* [italics added]. Policies that build on this assumption would be more effective and certainly less dehumanizing than the current system. (pp. 4-5)[3]

The theory in Table 4.4 may accomplish this. It employs the reciprocity principle to prescribe appropriate interactions among people who need help and people who are prepared to help. The first proposition establishes coverage of circumstances ignored by the ideological belief system. It claims that all interactions among people—the needy and non-needy alike—should be governed by the golden rule, "Do to others as you expect them to do to you."[4] Propositions 2 and 3 apply this rule to all the variations of adjustment possible in the free society.

Proposition 2 claims that prospects for self-determination are equal when all individuals respect each other's rights to self-determination. Proposition 3 claims

TABLE 4.4
The Fair Chances Theory

1. *Reciprocal Fairness.* In all societies, individuals treat others fairly when they are treated fairly.

2. *Freedom Through Equality.* In societies guaranteeing freedom for all, prospects for self-determination equalize when individuals respect each other's right to self-determination.

3. *Fair Chances for Freedom.* In a free society, individuals judge distributions of the self-determination experience to be fair when they have the same prospects for self-determination as others in that society.

4. *Conclusion.* Therefore, prospects for freedom are distributed fairly when all members of society have the same chance of engaging in their self-determined pursuits.

that individuals will judge their circumstances of freedom to be fair when they have the same chance of pursuing self-determined ends as others pursuing their self-determined ends.

According to this view of fairness, reciprocity is the basis of deciding what is fair in the free society. You and I have the same prospects for self-determination over the long term when we both judge our chances to be fair. Hence, fairness comes down to having an *equal chance or prospect* of engaging circumstances to reach ends that make life worthwhile. It is a condition that is conducive for self-directed action because the match between capacity and opportunity affects judgments about prospects for succeeding in a favored pursuit. When the match is equally optimal for all members of society, every person has the same prospects for experiencing the self-determined life. Every person is equally likely to use his or her capacity to alter circumstances associated with worthwhile ends.

A very attractive feature of the approach is its basis in reciprocity. I will support your right to act autonomously in pursuit of the good life as you define it if you support my right to do the same. Conversely, if your rights to self-determined action are threatened, I will support collective action to redress that unfair treatment, just as I expect you to support collective action to redress any unfair treatment abridging my right to self-determination. When we treat each other fairly—when we respect each other's rights to self-determination equally—we maintain a relationship of moral equals in society. Neither of us will suffer unfairly as one of us benefits unfairly. Proposition 4 concludes that prospects for self-determination are distributed fairly in society when all members have the same chance of living the self-determined life.

STEP 3: EVALUATING THE FAIR CHANCES THEORY

The purpose of this chapter was to find out if adopting self-regulation theory would require that we adjust existing beliefs about how to judge the unfavorable adjustment outcomes of needy people. Step 1 identified three discrepancies between those explanations and existing moral judgments. The first was between the labels used to judge people in need and the actual circumstances of adjustment responsible for those conditions. The second was between those labels and the principle of fairness. And the third was between the labels and the expectation of equal rights to self-determination.

Step 2 identified reasons for these inconsistencies. One reason was that the four theories of judgment were based on *assumptions* about how people adjust that had nothing to do with the actual outcomes they experience. This analysis suggested that the arguments for those beliefs may be coherent and valid but that they are nonetheless inconsistent with circumstances of need. Hence, they probably are not true. This alone should be sufficient to challenge the credibility of their claims about judging the needy.

Reflecting further on these analyses in Step 2 suggests that these belief claims also lack value. First of all, the four judgments they justify cannot fully account for the adjustment process. Hence, the beliefs lack significance. Second, they can only account for the needs of people who are victims, free riders, incompetents, or losers. Hence, they lack scope. Finally, the beliefs offer little guidance for deciding what should be done for people who do not fit these four need labels. Therefore, they lack utility. In short, ideological beliefs about judging needy people appear to be worthless because they lack value, and they appear to be suspect because they lack credibility.

Step 3 critiques the fair chances theory to determine if it is any better. This step evaluates credibility by assessing the theory's coherence, validity, and verifiability, and it evaluates worth by assessing the theory's significance, scope, and utility.

The Credibility Evaluation

To evaluate the theory's credibility, consider its four propositions in Table 4.4. The first proposition anchors judgments of fairness in the principle of reciprocity, "I will be fair with you because I expect you to be fair with me." Proposition 2 applies the principle of reciprocal fairness to the problem of freedom, claiming that prospects for self-determination equalize for different actors when people respect each other's rights to self-determination. A person agrees to respect another's prospects for self-determination if that other agrees to respect the person's prospects for self-determination. Proposition 3 claims that individuals who are free will judge their chances for expressing that freedom to be fair when their prospects for self-determination are equal. Proposition 4 concludes that prospects for freedom are distributed fairly when all members have the same chance to live the self-determined life.

To assess *coherence,* ask if the reasoning connecting the four propositions makes sense. Does the idea of fairness in the distribution of prospects for self-determination follow logically from the idea of fairness through reciprocity? If it does, then the theory is probably coherent. Next, judge the *validity* of the theory by asking if the conclusion in Proposition 4 can be deduced from Propositions 1 through 3. To check this, assume that one or more of the antecedent propositions is false, and then try to conclude that the claim in Proposition 4 is true. If you can, the theory is probably invalid. Drawing a conclusion without reference to supporting propositions suggests that the theory is invalid.

Last, examine the *truth* of the theory by determining how well the propositions match the circumstances they attempt to explain. Consider Proposition 1. Is it true in the sense of being consistent with the fair treatment experience of most people? Are individuals likely to treat each other fairly when they are treated fairly? Will you accept this as probably true, or do you want to run your own tests? Now turn to Proposition 2. Will free societies evolve toward equalized prospects for self-determination when every person respects every other person's rights? This is more difficult to evaluate, although on a small scale perhaps you can. Can you think of a way, or are you willing to accept the theory as probably true until contrary evidence suggests otherwise? Now consider Proposition 3. Is this true? The only way to know is to ask people how they judge different distributions of the freedom experience. Proposition 4 is similar and requires a similar test.

The Value Evaluation

The theory's value depends on your assessment of its significance, scope, and utility. Let us consider *significance* first. Remember that this theory binds all people together in an agreement to reciprocate fairness. Hence, your judgment about the fairness of our relationship is as important as my judgment about the fairness of our relationship. This claim appears to be more significant than ideological claims because it accounts for more variations in circumstances leading to unfair treatment. This is because it is responsive to every combination of capacity and opportunity that may affect a person's prospects for living the self-determined life. Any pattern that reduces prospects substantially from what others experience is grounds for receiving help. Is this a significant coverage of the problems of fair treatment that most people experience when attempting to live the self-determined life?

The second criterion for evaluating the theory's worth is *scope*. It assesses the theory's coverage of unfair circumstances. To examine this feature, consider the theory's focus on prospects for self-determination. For every condition of need, there is a judgment of fairness based on a comparison between a target actor's prospects and other actors' prospects. The assumption is that any actor at any time may experience higher or lower prospects than other actors. It raises a corresponding question of fairness that can provoke a judgment based on the new theory. Hence, you do not need to be a free rider, victim, loser, or incompetent to qualify for a judgment. Nor do you have to qualify as financially needy. This is because any substantive change in target actors' prospects compared to the average for everyone else in society evokes a fairness judgment. This is how the theory covers dramatic variations in need, fairness, and freedom. Is this sufficiently comprehensive to pass the scope test?

The third criterion for evaluating the theory's worth is *utility*. Is the theory useful in deciding what should be done about unusual adjustment outcomes in life? Proposition 4 claims that individuals will be dissatisfied with their situation when their unfavorable adjustment outcomes are due to prospects for self-determination that are less favorable than prospects of others in society. This information could be useful in deciding when and how to redress unmet needs. The next chapter will evaluate this feature of the theory. Perhaps the new knowledge it provides will guide social action toward appropriately redressing the hardship experienced in the free society. If it does, then the theory will have demonstrated its utility.

STEP 4: ADJUSTING BELIEFS

The last step of constructive theorizing asks if adopting this theory requires an adjustment in existing beliefs about what should be done, if anything, to ameliorate unfortunate adjustment outcomes. Recall that the previous chapter ended by asking the same question. At that time, we wanted to know if adopting the explanation for adjustment offered by self-regulation theory would require adjusting existing ideological beliefs about how to judge different adjustment outcomes. This provoked the theorizing in this chapter to produce the fair chances theory, which we will adopt and use in place of that ideological system of judgment. Now we must face the consequences of this change in our thinking. We must find out if adopting the fair chances theory will require changes in other beliefs we hold about *what should be done* about people who experience unusual adjustment outcomes in life. This is the question we will address next.

1. This problem was also discussed by Gans (1995) and by Katz (1989).

2. For a discussion on "freedom from" and "freedom to," see Gray (1991).

3. A similar point of view is presented in Davis (1995), Levitan, Gallo, and Shapiro (1993), and Sidel (1996).

4. For more on this claim and an update on the status of the principle, see Wattles (1996).

Policy Theorizing About Actions

ow we can use four-step theorizing to answer the question "What should be done for people in need?" It builds upon the theorizing in Chapter 3, which explained how things work for people in need, and the theorizing in Chapter 4, which explained how things should work for them. Our quest this time is to determine if the theories developed in these chapters are consistent with existing beliefs about what should be done to help them.

STEP 1: DEFINE THE DISCREPANCY

The first step in policy theorizing is the same as the first step in empirical and moral theorizing. It defines the problem as a discrepancy between circumstances and beliefs. Recall that Step 1 in Chapter 3 described the discrepancy between circumstances and beliefs about adjustment outcomes. Step 1 in Chapter 4 described the discrepancy between understanding those circumstances and beliefs about how to judge them. In this chapter, Step 1 describes inconsistencies between knowing about the fair chances judgments of adjustment outcomes and existing beliefs about what should be done about them. The four policy beliefs considered in this chapter are based on the political beliefs critiqued in the previous chapter: liberalism, conservatism, welfarism, and libertarianism.

Liberal Policy Theory

The first policy belief to consider receives its moral support from the liberal belief described in Table 4.1 of the previous chapter. Recall why that belief claimed that needy people deserved help. It claimed that they were victimized by opportunities denied them due to race or gender. The policy it implies asserts that majority members of society should assume *new obligations* with respect to minority members. They should act affirmatively by compensating members of those groups for their undeserved suffering. Affirmative action in the distribution of new opportunities in education and employment is an example of this policy. As Barbara Bergmann described it in *In Defense of Affirmative Action* (1996),

> Affirmative action is planning and acting to end the absence of certain kinds of people—those who belong to groups that have been subordinated or left out—from certain jobs and schools. It is an insurance company taking steps to break its tradition of promoting only white men to executive positions. It is the admissions office at the University of California at Berkeley seeking to boost the number of blacks in the freshman class beyond a smattering by looking for a few black kids who may not have learned to do well on multiple choice tests but are nevertheless very smart. It is a lily-white all-male trucking company hiring a black female driver and then coping with the anger of the other drivers. It is the Detroit police department striving to overcome the obstacles that capable blacks and women experience in making sergeant. (pp. 7-8)

According to Bergmann, affirmative action fights discrimination, reduces the harm caused by poverty associated with it, and promotes racial and gender diversity at all levels of society (pp. 9-10).

Is this approach to social redress consistent with the fair chances theory developed in the previous chapter? Will redistributing rights and responsibilities favoring left-out groups equalize their prospects for self-determination as justified by that theory? To answer these questions, consider some of the side effects of using group labels rather than individual circumstances to determine eligibility for compensatory opportunity. One effect is to provide compensating opportunities to people who may not deserve help because their prospects for self-determination are already favorable. Another effect is to ignore the needs of nongroup members whose prospects are not very favorable either. Is it fair to allow these side effects?

Conservative Policy Theory

Conservative policy is based on the conservative moral belief in Table 4.1 of the previous chapter. It claims that because people are free to conduct their own affairs in life, they should be held responsible for their actions. To guarantee equality of responsibility, society should provide incentives for responsible behavior and disincentives for irresponsible behavior. This is good for everyone over the long term, as Lawrence Mead (1986) asserted, because recently there has been "a sharp decline in the habits of competency and restraint that are essential to a humane society" (p. 1). The reason for it is that

> federal programs that support the disadvantaged and unemployed have been permissive in character, not authoritative. That is, they have *given benefits* to their recipients but have set few requirements for how they ought to function *in*

return. In particular, the programs have as yet no serious requirements that employable recipients work *in return* for support [italics added]. (p. 1)

Mead argued that existing policy awards benefits

essentially as entitlements, expecting next to nothing from the beneficiaries in return. The world recipients live in is economically depressed yet privileged in one sense, that it emphasizes their claims and needs almost to the exclusion of obligations. (p. 2)

Mead's policy solution requires that people in need do their part to help themselves: (a) They must work in available jobs if they are able-bodied; (b) they must contribute all they can to support their family; (c) they must be fluent and literate in English, whatever their native tongue may be; (d) they must learn enough in school to be employable; and (e) they must obey the law and respect the rights of others (p. 243). Mead justified these actions as follows:

What may be most disquieting about the idea of enforcing social obligations is the paternalism involved. Enforcement means more than just levying standards. It means local authorities instructing people how to behave. Government to some extent takes over the socializing role of parents. For teachers, whose clients are children, that role is explicit and noncontroversial. However, social workers, employment counselors, and other local staff often play the same role for adult recipients of welfare, employment, and training programs. They are more than clerks dispensing benefits. Through personal suasions, backed up by their official authority, they may try to motivate their clients to obey program rules, function better, and overcome problems. Necessarily, a more directive social policy would build up this authoritative role of local service provision. (p. 246)

Also supporting this view that no one should get something for nothing is the belief that people who work hard, obey the law, and take care of their families are being played for suckers. According to columnist William Raspberry (1996),

Our public discourse is full of talk about the harm welfare does to those who live on it. But isn't it likely that what we worry about privately is the possibility that our hard-earned money will be handed over to some well-fed woman who refuses to work—that we'll be played for suckers? I see the fear lurking behind virtually every public issue, from Social Security and health care reform to school vouchers and solid-waste recycling. Good ideas, maybe, but how can we be sure somebody's not out to take us for suckers? (p. A19)

This worry about being a sucker returns us to the question of obligations. Does Mead's equal responsibility expectation justify demanding that needy people assume greater responsibility for their own affairs (more obligations)? Will his policy improve or diminish their *prospects* for self-determination? Recall that the fair chances theory expects relationships among individuals to lead toward equal rights to self-determination among needy and non-needy alike. Will Mead's policy do this?

Welfarist Policy Theory

Now consider the welfarist policy, which is based on the moral justification in Table 4.1 of the previous chapter. According to this view, all members of society are of equal worth, even though some may lack the capacity to care for themselves. The policy action it recommends is for society to act on behalf of vulnerable people. Conditions of victimization and irresponsibility notwithstanding, society is still obligated to provide for the security of all to the maximum extent possible. Therefore, any circumstance that threatens a person's sense of well-being must be prevented or ameliorated. This is society's way of demonstrating that it values every person equally.

An example of this type of policy is Mickey Kaus's solution in *The End of Equality* (1992), which would protect needy people from the economic hardship they must endure due to their inability to succeed in the meritocracy. Kaus proposed a social structure that deemphasizes money competition and encourages public associations on the basis of equal worth.

> Instead of struggling against money-inegalitarian tides in the world economy over which American liberals have little control, it would make the most of a factor the government does have control over, namely the public sphere.
>
> The Civic Liberal idea is to use this public sphere to incubate and spread an egalitarian culture. Cultures don't fall from the sky. They come from institutions. The institutions of the private sphere, left unencumbered, will create their own culture, a culture in which money is likely to [be] the dominant, if not monolithic, determinant of status. We can keep reminding ourselves that there is an ineradicable element of chance in an entrepreneurial economy, that the Fairness Trap will never completely close, and that we have not and will not achieve the meritocratic equilibrium in which material reward corresponds perfectly to applied talent. But when money is the only game in town, it's hard not to follow the score.
>
> What's needed is another area of life with a different method of scoring. In the money sphere, after all, not *everyone* can succeed. But everyone, even the economy's losers, should be able to pass the test necessary for equal dignity in the public sphere. The institutions of that sphere would drive home the point of social equality—and the ultimate moral arbitrariness of capitalist success—through the crude expedient of treating all citizens equally and the more subtle tactic of providing a part of daily life actually enjoyed by various economic classes on this equal basis. (pp. 78-79)

Kaus claimed that this restructuring would encourage the mingling of individuals from all social classes. It would increase opportunities for egalitarian contacts through a universal military draft, political discussions, the seeking and receiving of health care, the securing of day care for children, and public transportation. He argued that

> we can have a health care system that almost everyone uses on an equal basis.
> . . . We can minimize the role of money in our democracy and maximize the time we spend in egalitarian political dialogue. We can frame our obligations so that rich and poor Americans serve the nation together. . . . We can have a society in which the various classes use the same subways and drop off their kid at the same day-care centers and run into each other at the post office. (p. 102)

Another approach to restructuring is John Rawls's plan in *A Theory of Justice* (1971). His approach would also protect vulnerable people from the harm created by egregious economic inequality. By claiming that the accumulation of material gain by some members of society is morally arbitrary, Rawls justified yoking economic gain produced by the most advantaged with a proportionate gain transferred to the most needy in society. The results that he promised were increased benefits for all as the fortunes of the few would improve and decreased income inequality separating the few from the many.

Both Kaus and Rawls aimed to protect the needy from hardship. Kaus aimed to protect them from social hardship, and Rawls aimed to protect them from economic hardship. Also, both of them assumed that because the needy are too incompetent to secure a share of the social and economic benefits through their own pursuits, some policy for institutional restructuring is necessary. Some version of a social security blanket is needed to cover the conditions of uncontrollable hardship that needy people inevitably experience.

Do you think these policies comply with the fair chances theory? Before answering, consider again the possible side effects. One is the effect of paternalistic protection on a person's sense of self-efficacy and the effect of that, in turn, on his or her judgments about pursuing self-defined ends in life. Extend this speculation further by considering the effect of this policy on the beliefs of non-needy individuals who come to think that people receiving protection are so incapable of acting on their own behalf that equalizing their prospects for self-determination is unimportant. How does this square with fair chances theory?

Libertarian Policy Theory

The last policy to examine is based on the libertarian belief about the needy described in Table 4.1 of the previous chapter. It assumes that all members of the free society have the right to keep what they earn, even though the consequence of expressing that right may separate people who succeed from people who do not. The only policy of help that it justifies is charity because approaches that mandate resource transfers to the unsuccessful violate property rights of the successful. Also, libertarians believe that any governmental intervention in private affairs is harmful, as David Boaz asserted in *Libertarianism: A Primer* (1997):

> In the recent discussion of cutting back on government welfare programs, many leading charities have warned that they can't assume all the responsibilities of government; they say they don't have that much money. Well, of course not. But the point is, the government programs have failed. The solution is not to replicate them. If government stopped encouraging irresponsibility, there would be less need for charity.... Across America there are thousands of small, local charitable organizations helping the poor. Americans give more than $125 billion and 20 billion hours a year to charity. If taxes were lower, and people understood that government was turning charitable responsibilities over to the civil society, they would give far more.
>
> If you're not convinced that private charity can replace government welfare, ask yourself this: Suppose you won $100,000 in a lottery. But there's a catch. You have to spend it to help the poor. Would you give it to the U.S. Department of Health and Human Services, your state human services agency, or a private charity? Most people would not hesitate to choose a private charity. (pp. 235-236)

Clearly, libertarian policy opposes any imposition of new obligations on the successful to aid the unsuccessful. If any obligations develop, they must come from individuals who decide for themselves they *ought to help.*

What do you think of this approach to helping the needy? Does it constitute fair treatment, and is it consistent with the fair chances theory? To answer, try to envision how charitable help may improve or hinder a needy person's prospects for living the self-determined life. Next, consider how it squares with the principle of reciprocity. Do you think people who are successful today would agree to be recipients of charity tomorrow if their fortunes changed and they experienced uncontrollable hardship? If you were to suffer this fate, would charity be sufficient to return you to the self-determined life? How do your answers match the expectation for equalized prospects?

STEP 2: FIND REASONS

This analysis suggests that the discrepancy problem we want to solve actually consists of four inconsistencies. The first is between fair chances theory and liberal policy theory, the second is between fair chances theory and conservative policy theory, the third is between fair chances theory and welfarist policy theory, and the fourth is between fair chances theory and libertarian policy theory. We will search for a way to explain all four at once.

Reasons for Existing Policies

One way to account for all of them is to find out how the four policies justify the imposition of new obligations on the non-needy or the needy. For example, what is the justification for the liberal policy of new obligations for the non-needy? What is the justification for the conservative policy of new obligations for the needy? What is the justification for the welfarist policy of new obligations for society? And what is the justification for the libertarian policy of no new obligations for the non-needy? By getting answers to these questions, we may be able to determine whether these changes will equalize prospects for self-determination between the needy and non-needy, as sanctioned by the fair chances theory. So let us examine the policy theories listed below to find some answers to these questions. I have reconstructed them from the assumptions and claims in Tables 4.1 through 4.3 of the previous chapter. You can do the same to see if my reconstructions are accurate.

Liberal Policy Theory

1. Some individuals experience unfair discrimination due to their status as members of minority groups in society.

2. This unfair discrimination creates unfair barriers to their self-determined pursuits.

3. These individuals cannot remove these barriers of unfair discrimination on their own.

4. Given that these individuals are not responsible for these social barriers, they are victims and deserve additional opportunities to overcome their unfortunate circumstances.

Conservative Policy Theory

1. In a society where every person is free and equal in his or her self-determined pursuits, individuals are responsible for their actions and the outcomes of those pursuits.

2. Some people abuse their freedom by avoiding this responsibility and expecting others to help them when they fail in their pursuits.

3. This is unfair to people who take responsibility for their actions and for the outcomes of their self-determined pursuits.

4. Therefore, all free riders, people who do not take responsibility for their actions and outcomes, should be required to take responsibility for their actions and the outcomes of their self-determined pursuits.

Welfarist Policy Theory

1. All members of society should be protected equally from unusual circumstances of hardship that are beyond their control.

2. Some individuals experience circumstances of hardship because they are helplessly incapable of improving their circumstances.

3. These people deserve to be protected from unusual circumstances because these conditions are beyond their control.

4. Therefore, all people in need who are helplessly incapable of controlling their circumstances deserve to be protected from the hardship and misery associated with those circumstances.[1]

Libertarian Policy Theory

1. In societies that maximize individual liberty by minimizing interference in individual pursuits, all persons have the same opportunity to get what they need and want in life.

2. When all persons have the same opportunity to get what they need and want in life, the distribution of those outcomes is fair, even though some individuals always tend to be more successful in producing favorable results than others.

3. Because any requirement that people who succeed help those who fail is an unfair interference with their freedom of pursuit, the only assistance that can be provided to people who fail is charity.

Does this list offer any clues as to the effects of these policies on prospects for self-determination for people in need? Liberal policy theory justifies the requirement that majority members give a portion of their opportunities to minority members because this is just compensation for past discrimination against minorities and their subsequent victimization. But will this equalize prospects for self-determination between the two groups? Conservative policy theory justifies the demand that the needy do more to help themselves because this equalizes responsibility for all members of society. But will this equalize their prospects for self-determination as well? Welfare policy theory justifies protecting people who are incapacitated by their circumstances because this is the only way their suffering can be ameliorated to the maximum extent possible. Will this bring their prospects for self-determination in line with those of people who do not suffer comparable hardship? And libertarian policy theory justifies giving charitable contributions to the needy because this is the only type of help that does not unjustly require the non-needy to give. But again, will this equalize prospects for self-determination between the needy and non-needy?

Answering these questions is difficult because we know from fair chances theory that policies of help should respond to *actual circumstances* of hardship and should be consistent with the *principle of reciprocity*. Therefore, for the sake of their credibility and worth, these policy theories should offer some empirical assurance that the people they cover are in fact victimized by discrimination, behaving irresponsibly, helplessly overcome by their hardship, or losers in the fair free market exchange (the actual circumstances criterion). They should also offer an assurance that *any* person anticipating one of these difficulties would agree to its treatment and corresponding label (the reciprocity criterion). Given these provisos, there might be a chance that these policies would equalize prospects between needy and non-needy and hence be consistent with the fair chances theory.

The problem is that such assurances are highly improbable, given that so many people in need do not fit in any *one* of these ideological niches of need. We know from previous chapters that people's circumstances vary from time to time depending on where they are in their lives and their circumstances. A person may be eligible for the liberal's victim label at one time, for the conservative's free-rider label at another time, for the welfarist's hopelessly helpless label at a third point in her life, and for the libertarian's loser label on a fourth occasion. And on all other occasions, the same needy person may find him- or herself outside these categories of need and hence ineligible for any help at all.

Figure 5.1 illustrates the many eligibility problems created by ideological assumptions about fixed capacity and responsibility. The four overlapping circles within the large circle represent the definitional overlap that is at the heart of many ideological debates about what should be done to help. Overlaps 1 through 4 in the diagram indicate debates between liberals and conservatives (Area 1), between conservatives and libertarians (Area 2), between libertarians and welfarists (Area 3), and between welfarists and liberals (Area 4).

Here are some examples of overlapped definitions in dispute. Liberals argue that students with disabilities should be excused for the outrageous behavior that results from their disability, whereas conservatives argue that the conduct of all students should conform to school rules and the law (Area 1). Conservatives claim that the law prohibits gay men or lesbians from marrying each other, whereas libertarians claim that nothing should interfere with their freedom to do as they wish, given that they harm no one (Area 2). Libertarians argue that people in need suffer because they lose out in the free market exchange for economic gain, whereas welfarists argue that the needy are incapable of taking care of themselves (Area 3). Welfarists claim that disabled people are incapable of working and hence need social security protection, whereas liberals claim that they

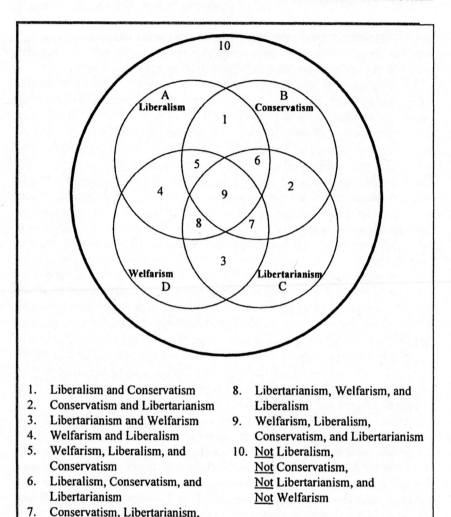

1. Liberalism and Conservatism
2. Conservatism and Libertarianism
3. Libertarianism and Welfarism
4. Welfarism and Liberalism
5. Welfarism, Liberalism, and
   Conservatism
6. Liberalism, Conservatism, and
   Libertarianism
7. Conservatism, Libertarianism,
   and Welfarism

8. Libertarianism, Welfarism, and
   Liberalism
9. Welfarism, Liberalism,
   Conservatism, and Libertarianism
10. <u>Not</u> Liberalism,
    <u>Not</u> Conservatism,
    <u>Not</u> Libertarianism, and
    <u>Not</u> Welfarism

FIGURE 5.1. Definitional Overlap Between Liberalism, Conservatism, Libertarianism, and Welfarism

can work and that discrimination in employment prevents them from finding decent jobs (Area 4).

Ideological policy disputes also occur diagonally in the diagram. Liberals, for example, argue that affirmative action is necessary because people in need are victims of discrimination, whereas libertarians argue that meritorious advancement is necessary because society needs the best people in the highest-ranking jobs (Area 9). And welfarists argue that women and children are the most deserving of protection because they are always vulnerable when left on their own, whereas conservatives argue that ordinary tax-paying people need protection from needy people who refuse to help themselves and their families (Area 9).

At the epicenter of these disputes is, of course, the basic contradiction between the claims of ideologues who argue that one label fits all needy people and the fact that one needy person can fit all four labels (Area 9). A disabled person, for example, can qualify for social security support under the protection of a welfare policy and for job opportunity compensation under the antidiscrimination protection of a liberal policy. That same person can also be subjected to the rebuke of the conservative who believes that he or she uses the disability to excuse his or her failures to get along in life, and to the patronizing sympathy of the libertarian who believes that the disability explains why he or she will never succeed in the meritorious competition for a valuable position in society.

Explanation for a New Policy

The fact that the same person can meet one, some, all, or none of these definitions of need reflects variability in individual circumstances rather than definitional sensitivity of ideological labeling. Consider this very credible case of variation in need, which mocks all these ideological disputes over how to label every needy person. A person is suddenly disabled and for a brief period hopelessly helpless. For that moment in her life, the welfarist definition of need is appropriate, along with its policy of protection. Following a period of recovery, however, the same person seeks work and discovers that her former employer has discriminated against her because of her new condition. So she challenges that treatment, with support from liberals who cite the Americans with Disabilities Act to justify compensating her with back pay and a job. Years later, she tires of working and decides to return to Social Security by reclaiming hardship due to her disability. But after she quits work, conservative policy makers discover her past and institute disincentives so that she will return to work and take responsibility for her life as she once did. This motivates her to return to work.

What makes this case plausible is our knowledge about this person's changing capacities and opportunities, not the ideological system that insisted on labeling her as hopelessly helpless, a victim, or a free rider. Although *none* of these policies could respond to all of her needs as they changed over time, her changing needs could satisfy the assumptions of the *different policies* that affected her life. This explains why ideological help is so limited in its coverage of people in need. It takes *all four competing policies* to cover *some needs,* yet *many needs* are not covered by *any competing policy.*

This conclusion comes as no surprise, given what we know from self-regulation theory about how we adjust to change. Our capacity (resources) and opportunities (favorable circumstances relative to capacity) to adjust are naturally variable. Interactions between these factors determine the probability that we will alter circumstances according to our plans and goals. Hence, there is no fixed capacity-opportunity condition reflecting our adjustments to all situations. Every combination of capacity (resources) and opportunity (circumstances) is different, as is every judgment about prospects for success. Prospects for self-determination, which are also a function of these judgments, also vary from person to person and situation to situation.

This view offers a fresh perspective on what it means to have a fair chance to act on the right to self-determination. Two people have the same chance for self-determination when Person A's judgments about what he can accomplish given his capacity and opportunity are roughly the same as Person B's judgments about what she can accomplish given her capacity and opportunity. Person A and Person B have the same prospects for self-determination when they judge their chances of acting on their circumstances and getting what they need and want to be the same. They are fairly situated in their respective circumstances (with respect to their different conditions of capacity and opportunity) because Person A's chances (prospects or probability) of acting on his circumstances are the same as Person B's chances of acting on her circumstances. The two have an equal or fair chance of acting in their own interests—of being self-determined—in that particular comparison situation.

This is how the fair chance condition relates to the actual circumstances of a person's adjustment. A fair chance is present when these capacity-opportunity matches for different individuals yield comparable prospects for self-determination across different individuals, substantial time periods, and different material and social situations. When prospects are comparable on average across different persons and circumstances, everyone has roughly the same chance of acting in a self-determined manner. People have roughly the same probability of engaging their circumstances to reach their own goals throughout their lifetime, for example.

This understanding is not reflected in the four ideological policy theories. This is because liberal theory is based upon the assumption that need is a function of *fixed* patterns of *equal capacity* and *unequal opportunity*. Conservative policy theory is based upon the assumption that need is a function of *fixed* patterns of *equal capacity* and *equal opportunity*. Welfarist policy theory is based upon the assumption that need is a function of *fixed* patterns of *unequal capacity* and *unequal opportunity*. And libertarian policy theory is based upon the assumption that need is a function of *fixed* patterns of *unequal capacity* and *equal opportunity*.

Now we know why ideological help can only cover that limited area of undisputed needs identified as Areas A, B, C, and D of Figure 5.1: because when needs fall into overlapping Areas 1 through 7, ideologues debate about what they are and how they should be treated, again according to their fixed conceptions of hardship and its amelioration. Then, when circumstances change again to exclude a person from the covered areas in the diagram, debate ceases because now the person does not qualify for any kind of help. Now he or she is left out of the circled areas altogether (Area 10).

This clarifies the need for a policy theory that covers these variable conditions of hardship in a way that is consistent with fair chances theory constructed in Chapter 4 and with the self-regulation theory of adjustment constructed in Chapter 3. Such a theory would have to prescribe social action in a way that was consistent with the dynamics between capacity and opportunity that affect a person's prospects for self-determination. It would also have to direct policy toward equalizing prospects for self-determination for all people.

The theory of equal opportunity may fit these specifications. It is consistent with the fair chances theory because it is based on the premise that in a free society all persons have the right to self-determination. Hence, when any circumstance prevents some members from expressing their right, society has an obligation to intervene to equalize prospects for self-determination.

Equal Opportunity Theory

1. All individuals have the right to self-determination.

2. All societies have some individuals who lack the capacity to self-determine.

3. All societies generate unequal opportunities to self-determine.

4. Consequently, some individuals do not experience the right to self-determine because they lack the capacity and opportunity to do so.

5. Therefore, all societies should optimize prospects for self-determination among these least advantaged members by increasing their capacity and improving their opportunity to self-determine. (Mithaug, 1996, p. 11)

STEP 3: EVALUATE THE THEORY

This step of constructive theorizing evaluates the credibility and worth of this new theory. It employs the same six criteria that evaluated the self-regulation theory in Chapter 3 and the fair chances theory in Chapter 4. Again, credibility depends on the theory's coherence, validity, and verifiability, and worth depends on its significance, scope, and utility.

Is the Theory Credible?

Begin by examining the theory's *coherence.* Ask if the reasons offered to explain the discrepancy between the right and the experience of self-determination make sense. First, consider Propositions 2 and 3, which identify the factors affecting the experience of self-determination: a person's capacity and opportunity to self-determine. Do these two propositions connect Propositions 1 and 4 in a logical manner? To answer, let us assume that Propositions 2 and 3 are true. Now ask if they explain why the experience of self-determination can be discrepant from the right to self-determination, as claimed in Proposition 4. Imagine, for example, what happens when people lack the capacity or the opportunity to self-determine. Does it make sense to claim that this will affect their experience of self-determination? If it does, then the argument is probably coherent.

Now consider the theory's *validity.* Does the conclusion in Proposition 5 follow from the premises in Propositions 1 through 4? If Propositions 1 through 4 are true, for example, is the conclusion in Proposition 5 likely to be true? Does the universal right to self-determination in Proposition 1 plus the conditions required to experience that right as identified in Propositions 2 through 4 obligate the collective to help people lacking the experience of self-determination, as concluded in Proposition 5?

Another way of assessing validity is to ask if the conclusion in Proposition 5 follows logically even if one or more of the other propositions is false. For example, if we assume that there is no right to self-determination (Proposition 1 is not true), is it still logical to conclude from the premises that society has an obligation to help people lacking the experience of self-determination? Conduct the same test for Proposition 2. If it is false that some individuals in society lack the capacity to self-determine, does it make sense to claim in Proposition 5 that society has an obligation to increase the capacity of persons lacking the experience of self-determination? Do the same test for Proposition 3. Assume that it is false that societies do not generate unequal opportunities to self-determine. Then ask if it is logical to conclude that society has an obligation to improve opportunities for the needy. Finally, conduct this test for Proposition 4 by assuming that it is false that individuals lack the experience of the right to self-determination because they lack the capacity or opportunity to self-determine. Does this change the truth status of Proposition 5 that society has an obligation to optimize prospects for self-determination for those least advantaged members?

In summary, if any of these propositions is false, you would expect the conclusion to be false as well. If you can argue logically that one or more of these propositions is false but that the conclusion is true nonetheless, then the argument is probably invalid. This does not mean Proposition 5 is untrue. It only means Proposition 5 cannot be inferred from Propositions 1 through 4. The theory is valid only if its conclusion is consistent with those propositions. Does the theory offer a valid argument for what a free society ought to do when people lack the capacity or opportunity to self-determine? Are you willing to conclude that this theory presents a valid argument?

To assess the third credibility criterion, ask if the propositions of the theory are *verifiable*. Think about what you might have to do to verify their claims. Consider the proposition that all members of a society have the right to self-determination. Can you verify this assertion? If you live in the United States, you can perhaps test it by examining the Declaration of Independence, the Constitution, and the Bill of Rights. Ask the same question of Propositions 2 through 4. Can you test Proposition 2? You can if you can assess the capacity levels of individuals to determine if the resources they have under their control affect their levels of self-determination. You can test the claim in Proposition 3 if you can determine whether the distribution of opportunities among different individuals, such as access to education and jobs, also affects their levels of self-determination. You can test the claim in Proposition 4 by determining if the lack of capacity (limited resources) *and* opportunities (access to education and jobs, for example) affects people's *judgments* about their prospects for engaging in self-determined pursuits. If results indicate that conditions of lowered capacity and unfavorable opportunities produce judgments of lowered prospects for self-determination, Proposition 4 is probably supported. In summary, results from these inquiries could support or refute the claims in Propositions 1 through 4. Hence, those propositions are verifiable. Their truth values can be determined.

Now consider Proposition 5. Can it be verified? Is it possible to enact a social policy to increase the capacity and opportunity of people in need and then to assess their levels of self-determination? If it is, then any change in prospects for self-determination following the enactment of the equal opportunity policy could support or refute the theory.

Is the Theory Valuable?

To answer questions about the worth of equal opportunity theory, determine if it is significant, comprehensive, and useful. The theory is significant if it fully eliminates the discrepancy between the fair chances theory of judgment and existing beliefs about what should be done about people in need. Stated another way, it is significant if it fully explains what should be done about the circumstances judged unfair by the fair chances theory.

One approach to this evaluation is to examine those assumptions about capacity and opportunity that rendered ideological policy theories inconsistent with the fair chances theory. They assumed capacity and responsibility to be fixed. Equal opportunity theory, by contrast, assumes capacity and opportunity to be variable. This allows the theory's prescriptions for help to take into account variations in a person's capacity and opportunities to achieve what he or she wants in life.

To illustrate, let us assume that at one period in his life, a person has the resources (capacity) and circumstances (opportunity) necessary to sustain the achievement of desirable outcomes. But at another point, his reduced resources (capacity) and increased obstacles (opportunities) produce unfavorable prospects for maintaining himself as he once did. According to equal opportunity theory, this person is not eligible for help during the first period but is eligible for help during the second. This sensitivity to his *changing needs* is reflected in Proposition 4, which states that persistent patterns of limited capacity and unfavorable opportunity may affect his experience of self-determination. According to Proposition 5, this may obligate the collective to redress his unfortunate circumstance. This prescription for help is consistent with fair chances theory in that *any condition* judged unfair by fair chances theory is justification to equalize prospects. In this sense, equal opportunity theory appears to answer all questions of not knowing what should be done about circumstances judged to be bad or wrong by the fair chances theory. Do you agree?

Now let us consider the theory's *scope,* which requires an examination of the range of unfortunate adjustment experiences redressed by its policy. Recall from Step 2 how existing policy theories were limited in their coverage. Liberal policies covered only victims of discrimination. Conservative policies covered only free riders. Welfarist policies covered only incompetents. And libertarian policies covered only losers. Equal opportunity theory can cover a full range of needy people because it prescribes interventions to ameliorate patterns of capacity-opportunity interaction that unfairly diminish *any* person's prospects for self-determination. Covered individuals include people who are poor, victimized by discrimination, economically disadvantaged, or incapacitated due to physical, mental, or emotional disability. This coverage is comprehensive in the sense that any condition of capacity and opportunity adversely affecting prospects for self-determination justifies assistance. Can you think of a category of need not covered by the theory's prescriptions? If you can, then you probably can make a counterclaim regarding its scope.

The last criterion for evaluating the theory's worth is *utility*. This standard provokes us to ask if the redress prescribed by Proposition 5, for example, is helpful in guiding social action to ameliorate the unusual hardship that some people experience. A review of social policies constructed in the last half of this century suggests that perhaps it does. The following passage from *Equal Opportunity Theory* (Mithaug, 1996) describes this development and how it relates to fair chances:

> When prospects for pursuing the good in life are distributed unequally among individuals and groups, fairness conceived collectively and comparatively is

threatened. This is troubling and is likely to provoke social change in the direction of fairness.

According to equal opportunity theory, this provocation for redress is stimulus for social change in the direction of the optimal prospects principle. This is what is happening today. Even in the midst of widespread disappointment about the pattern of social reform of past decades, there is the persistent, nagging reminder to be fair. This translates into increased clarity of purpose in recommending social redress. The issue today is one of fair chances, not one of equal outcomes. Policymakers are less likely to confuse a prospect or chance with a gain or an outcome because their focus is on *prospects* not gains. For students of color and students with disabilities, the expectation is for both to receive a fair chance at getting an education. It is not that they be guaranteed an educational outcome. No one deserves a guarantee. The same holds for people on welfare. The expectation for them is the same—to have a fair chance at pursuing opportunity for personal gain; it is not to receive a guaranteed level of support because no one in society deserves that. In other words, the focus on equal chances or equal prospects is a focus on the *means* individuals need to pursue opportunity that incurs a reasonable risk but promises a reasonable gain toward those ends in life they desire. (pp. 232-233)

To test the utility of this theory in a very practical way, ask if its prescriptions for social redress offer a viable alternative to the solutions to unmet need offered by policies like welfare, affirmative action, and special education. How does its method of redress compare with those policies?

STEP 4: ADJUST BELIEFS

The last step in constructive theorizing adjusts other beliefs that may be inconsistent with this view about what should be done to ameliorate the hardship of people in need. Recall our response to this step in Chapter 3 after constructing self-regulation theory to explain how things work for people in need. It was to examine existing beliefs about how things ought to work for people in need. This led to the adjustment in Chapter 4 that produced the fair chances theory, which in turn provoked inquiries about what should be done for people in need. We answered these questions by constructing the equal opportunity theory in this chapter. Now we are back to Step 4, asking the same question again. What additional beliefs must be adjusted to accommodate this new theory? Having completed a cycle of theorizing about how things work (Chapter 3), how things ought to work (Chapter 4), and what should be done (Chapter 5), we ask one more time if there is anything left to theorize about.

Perhaps there is just one more thing to consider. This is the possibility that actions taken to fulfill the prescriptions of equal opportunity theory will produce results that are inconsistent with expectations to equalize prospects for self-determination. If this happens, you may be provoked into theorizing again about how things work, how they ought to work, and what should be done about them. You may find yourself engaged in another round of theorizing, which leads to yet another round, and yet another. Then you may ask, when will it finally end?

NOTE

1. For a detailed discussion of a theory on protecting the vulnerable, see Goodin (1985, 1988).

Conclusion

To conclude this book, let us review major points about constructive theorizing, summarize the five chapters, and get you started theorizing on your own. There are four main points to keep in mind when using the strategy to construct a new explanation about something. The first is that theorizing is *always a reaction* to a provocative circumstance that is *inconsistent* with a belief or theory you hold about how things work, how they ought to work, or what should to be done about them. It is why you think and reason to discover something new. It is your reason for theorizing. Its contrasting condition, the absence of the troubling event, is knowing all you need and want to satisfy your interests and pursue your ends. It is having all the theories and beliefs you need for these purposes. Consequently, any *change in these conditions* from knowing to not knowing something due to a failure in your beliefs or theories is likely to provoke you to seek new answers and construct new explanations.

The second point is that constructive theorizing is simply a *thinking strategy* for reacting to this change from knowing to not knowing something important to you. It has four steps to resolve such problems: (a) defining the discrepancy between understanding and not understanding the unusual event or circumstance, (b) finding reasons and constructing explanations for what is not understood, (c) evaluating those reasons and explanations, and (d) adjusting existing beliefs accordingly.

The third point is that this strategy applies to three types of questions about not knowing something: factual questions about how things work, value questions about how they ought to work, and action questions about what should be done about them. And the results of these types of inquiries are empirical theories, moral theories, and policy theories.

The fourth point is that constructive theorizing is like everyday problem solving that is also provoked by unexpected events. I have emphasized this point throughout the book to reduce its mystery. Theorizing need not be reserved for profound ivory tower thinkers because anyone with capacity to solve problems can do it well. It is simply a way of thinking clearly about why events occur, what their moral significance is, and what should be done about them.

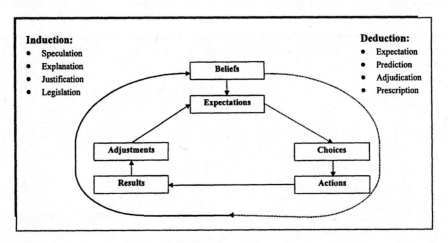

FIGURE 6.1. Constructive Theorizing as Problem Solving in Order to Make Adjustments

The first chapter was devoted almost exclusively to explaining the practical features of constructive theorizing. It showed how this approach to solving problems of not understanding something resembles general problem solving, practical reasoning, and self-regulated learning. The chapter also explained that this strategy is different from them because it always produces a theory, always evaluates the credibility and worth of the result, and never produces final solutions to problems of not knowing something. Figure 6.1 illustrates some of these features by showing how expectations, choices, actions, and evaluations function during the inductive and deductive phases of theorizing. The chapter ended by using the method to solve the problem of not knowing why a disabled golfer requested a cart for a PGA tournament. The result was an empirical theory explaining why Casey Martin requested a cart, a moral theory explaining whether he was right to request the cart, and a policy theory explaining whether that request should be granted.

Chapter 2 made the claim that everyone, including you, prefers credible and valuable beliefs to beliefs that are suspect or useless. Then it employed constructive theorizing to resolve the apparent contradiction between this claim and the fact that many people hold beliefs that lack credibility or value. The theory produced by this round of theorizing explained that people whose beliefs are inadequate probably do not know it. In addition, people who know that their beliefs are inadequate but hold them anyway probably do not know how to evaluate and improve them. Hence, they are stuck with beliefs that do not help them adjust optimally to life's unusual circumstances. In the course of developing this explanation, the chapter also showed how six criteria for evaluating a theory's credibility and worth guide decisions about adopting and using one theory rather than another.

Chapters 3 through 5 demonstrated the functional linkage between empirical, moral, and policy theorizing about three questions of not knowing something: Why do some people experience unusually unfavorable adjustment outcomes in life? How should we judge those unusual adjustment outcomes? What should we do about them? This series of demonstrations showed that although the *content* of these questions changed during empirical, moral, and policy reasoning, the *method* of theorizing remained the same—four-step theorizing.

Chapter 3, "Empirical Theorizing About Facts," constructed self-regulation theory to explain these unfortunate circumstances, which in turn created a problem of not knowing how to judge those circumstances. Chapter 4, "Moral Theorizing About Values" constructed the fair chances theory to solve this problem, which in turn created a new problem of not knowing what to do about those circumstances. Chapter 5, "Policy Theorizing About Actions," constructed equal opportunity theory to solve this problem. The chapter ended by suggesting that theorizing was unlikely to end there. This is because prescriptions for action emanating from equal opportunity theory could, for example, produce results that would be inconsistent with the explanation for adjustment provided by self-regulation theory. And this, in turn, could provoke more theorizing. The recursive nature of this method of theorizing is illustrated again in Figure 6.2.

THEORIZING ON YOUR OWN

Now it is your turn to use this strategy to theorize about unusual circumstances that you do not understand. To help you get started, I have identified three problems that you can use to begin constructing your own empirical, moral, and policy theories. The first is about disabled athletes seeking equal opportunities in competitive sports, the second is about the accelerating universe, and the third is about cloning. All three were reported in the *New York Times* from 1997 to 1999. Table 6.1 lists 4 articles on disabled athletes, Table 6.2 lists 7 articles on the accelerating universe, and Table 6.3 lists 14 articles on cloning. I used them to construct an empirical, moral, and policy theory for each problem. The theories and the steps leading to their construction are in Appendix A.

Before turning to that appendix to check those results, collect the articles listed in the table and any others that have appeared since. Read them until you feel you have sufficient background to theorize on your own. Then use the four steps of the strategy to construct your own theories. Table 6.4 provides a checklist to follow so you can keep track of where you are in the process. When you finish and are satisfied with your results, turn to Appendix A to compare them

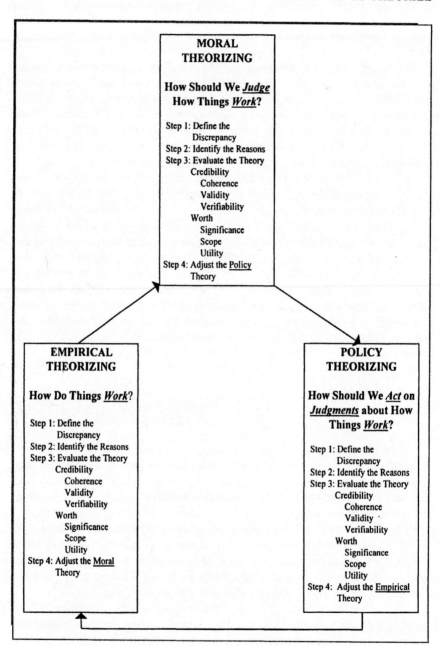

FIGURE 6.2. Recursive Theorizing to Solve an Empirical, Moral, and Policy Problem

---

TABLE 6.1

Background for Theorizing
About Athletes With Disabilities

---

1. Nobles, C. (1997, January 12). Allowed to use a cart for now, golfer wins Nike tour event. *New York Times*.

2. Fields, B. (1999, October 24). Casey Martin earns a spot on PGA tour. *The New York Times*.

3. McKinley, J. C., Jr. (1999, November 4). Wheelchair racers seek equality with runners. *New York Times*.

4. McKinley, J. C., Jr. (1999, November 8). No stop signs on the course: Also, no prizes at the end of it. *New York Times*.

TABLE 6.2

Background for Theorizing
About the Accelerating Universe

---

1. Wilford, J. N. (1998, January 9). New data suggest universe will expand forever. *New York Times*.

2. Wilford, J. N. (1998, March 3). Wary astronomers ponder an accelerating universe. *New York Times*.

3. Johnson, G. (1998, March 8). Once upon a time, there was a big bang theory. *New York Times*.

4. Browne, M. W. (1998, March 12). Asteroid is expected to make a pass close to earth in 2028. *New York Times*.

5. Wilford, J. N. (1998, May 5). Cosmologists ponder "missing energy" of the universe. *New York Times*.

6. Browne, M. W. (1998, June 6). Finances worry neutrino researchers. *New York Times*.

7. Browne, M. W. (1998, June 5). Mass found in elusive particle: Universe may never be the same. *New York Times*.

TABLE 6.3

Background for Theorizing About Cloning

1. Kolata, G. (1997, February 23). Scientist reports first cloning ever of adult mammal. *New York Times.*

2. Kolata, G. (1997, February 23). With cloning of sheep, the ethical ground shifts. *New York Times.*

3. Fisher, L. M. (1997, February 24). Cloned animals offer companies faster path to new drugs. *New York Times.*

4. Bell, D. A. (1997, March 2). To the editor. *New York Times.*

5. Maranto, G. (1997, March 2). To the editor. *New York Times.*

6. Seelye, K. Q. (1997, March 5). Clinton bans federal money for efforts to clone humans. *New York Times.*

7. Kolata, G. (1997, June 8). Ethics panel recommends a ban on human cloning. *New York Times.*

8. Kolata, G. (1997, December 2). On cloning humans, "never" turns swiftly into "why not." *New York Times.*

9. Tribe, L. H. (1997, December 5). Second thoughts on cloning. *New York Times.*

10. Kolata, G. (1998, January 8). Proposal for human cloning draws dismay and disbelief. *New York Times.*

11. A cloning plan leads to vows to outlaw it. (1998, January 12). *New York Times.*

12. Caplan, A. L. (1998, January 28). Why the rush to ban cloning? *New York Times.*

13. Kolata, G. (1998a, March 13). Congress is cautioned against ban on human-cloning work. *New York Times.*

14. Kolata, G. (1998, July 23). In big advance, cloning creates 50 mice. *New York Times.*

with mine. Don't be disappointed if they are different. This doesn't mean that your theories are wrong or that my theories are. It just means we theorized differently, perhaps by focusing on different information or by thinking differently about it. However, by using these differences or inconsistencies between our theories, you can theorize again to improve the credibility or value of both. Once you do this, you will have done everything I did in the theorizing examples pre-

TABLE 6.4

The Constructive Theorizing Checklist

Empirical Theorizing: How Does It Work?	*Completed?*
Step 1: Define the discrepancy between what you know and what you don't know.	_____
Step 2: Identify reasons and construct a theory that lists those reasons.	_____
Step 3: Evaluate the theory.	
Is it credible?	
Are the reasons coherent?	_____
Is the conclusion valid?	_____
Is the theory verifiable?	_____
Is it valuable?	
Is the theory significant?	_____
Is the theory comprehensive?	_____
Is the theory useful?	_____
Step 4: Adjust the moral theory.	_____
Identify the moral circumstances that may be affected by this theory, and	

GO TO

Moral Theorizing: How to Judge How It Works?	
Step 1: Define the discrepancy between what you know and what you don't know.	_____
Step 2: Identify reasons and construct a theory that lists those reasons.	_____
Step 3: Evaluate the theory.	
Is it credible?	
Are the reasons coherent?	_____
Is the conclusion valid?	_____
Is the theory verifiable?	_____
Is it valuable?	
Is the theory significant?	_____
Is the theory comprehensive?	_____
Is the theory useful?	_____
Step 4: Adjust the moral theory.	_____
Identify the actions that may be affected by the empirical and moral theory, and	

GO TO

Policy Theorizing: How to Act on Judgments About How It Works?	
Step 1: Define the discrepancy between what you know and what you don't know.	_____
Step 2: Identify reasons and construct a theory that lists those reasons.	_____
Step 3: Evaluate the theory.	
Is it credible?	
Are the reasons coherent?	_____
Is the conclusion valid?	_____
Is the theory verifiable?	_____
Is it valuable?	
Is the theory significant?	_____
Is the theory comprehensive?	_____
Is the theory useful?	_____
Step 4: Adjust the empirical theory.	_____
Identify the circumstances affected by this policy theory, and	

RETURN TO *Empirical Theorizing*

sented in this book. You will be well on your way to developing the skills of a good theorizer.

PROBLEM 1: ELITE ATHLETES WITH DISABILITIES

Recently, elite athletes with disabilities have challenged the status quo in sporting events by demanding accommodations in rules and practice that will improve their chances for successful participation. In professional golf, Casey Martin demanded that the PGA alter its must-walk rule so he could use a golf cart to travel from hole to hole. In New York, wheelchair racers demanded that the city's marathon establish a separate but equal division for wheelchair racers only. Both requests have received moral if not legal support from the Americans with Disabilities Act, which prohibits discrimination against persons with disabilities. The two cases present difficult empirical, moral, and policy questions because they challenge popular views about who the best athletes are and what constitutes fair competition among them.

PROBLEM 2: THE ACCELERATING UNIVERSE

Most astronomers and cosmologists believe the universe is the product of one big, primordial bang or explosion that propelled universal matter outward in an expansion that is gradually slowing. They also believe that this expansion will eventually cease and that ultimately the universe may even contract (implode) due to the gravitational pull on matter. This belief (theory) has generated predictions about the rate of expansion as measured by the changing positions of various celestial bodies. Recent observations have produced findings that contradict this prediction of a decelerating expansion. Dr. Adam Riess from the University of California at Berkeley claims that the expansion rate today is about 15% greater than it was 7 billion years ago (Wilford, 1998c). This is troubling because it challenges a long-held belief about the nature of the universe. It raises significant empirical, moral, and policy questions that demand answers.

PROBLEM 3: CLONING A NEW EWE

An unexpected biological event occurred on February 23, 1997, when the media reported that scientists had succeeded in cloning an adult mammal. This was unusual because many believed that DNA could not be introduced into an adult cell to create genetically identical embryos. Dr. Ian Wilmut, an embryologist at the Roslin Institute in Edinburgh, took a mammary cell from an adult sheep and then manipulated its DNA so that the egg from another adult sheep would accept the DNA and subdivide to duplicate the genetic material as if it were its own. This produced a perfectly normal fertilized egg that was implanted into another ewe to produce a lamb named Dolly. Tests showed that Dolly was the clone of the adult ewe that supplied its DNA (Kolata, 1997d).

REVIEWING CLAIMS, TERMS, PROCESSES

In preparation for your solo at theorizing, review the following material, which includes the claims of constructive theorizing, the theories constructed in the book, and the terms used to describe their construction. The main claims of constructive theorizing are as follows:

1. Inconsistencies between circumstances and beliefs create a need to adjust beliefs by improving their correspondence with circumstances or to adjust circumstances by improving their correspondence with beliefs (Chapter 1).

2. Constructive theorizing is a method of solving problems of not knowing how to reconcile beliefs with unusual material and social circumstances (Chapter 1).

3. Given that constructive theorizing is solving problems of not knowing why a circumstance is inconsistent with a belief and given that all people solve problems of adjustment, all people theorize to learn why circumstances are inconsistent with their beliefs (Chapter 1).

4. Given that problems of adjustment to unusual circumstances can be solved in four steps, problems of not knowing how to adjust beliefs can be solved in four steps (Chapter 1).

5. The four steps of problem solving are: (a) Define the problem as a discrepancy between the goal state and the actual state, (b) find a procedure that will reduce the discrepancy, (c) use the procedure to determine if it reduces or eliminates the discrepancy, (d) repeat the steps until the discrepancy is eliminated (Chapter 1).

6. The four steps of constructive theorizing are similar: (a) Define the problem as a discrepancy between the goal state of knowing why a belief is inconsistent with a circumstance and the actual state of not knowing why the belief is inconsistent with the circumstance, (b) find reasons and construct an explanation that will reduce the discrepancy between knowing and not knowing why the belief is inconsistent with the circumstance, (c) evaluate the credibility and value of the explanation to determine if it adequately reduces the discrepancy between knowing and not knowing, (d) adopt the explanation and adjust other beliefs that are inconsistent with the new belief by repeating the steps (Chapters 1-5).

7. The three problems of not knowing why beliefs are inconsistent with circumstances are (a) empirical problems of not knowing the cause of a circumstance, (b) moral problems of not knowing how to judge a circumstance, and (c) policy problems of not knowing what to do about a circumstance (Chapter 1).

8. Beliefs influence adjustments to circumstances by generating expectations, which influence choices, which influence actions on those circumstances (Chapter 2).

9. Beliefs suggest relationships between expectations, choices, actions, and results (Chapter 2).

10. The motivation to theorize is created by the *discrepancy* between wanting to know why a circumstance is inconsistent with a belief and not knowing the reasons for the inconsistency (Chapter 2).

11. The problem of not knowing the reasons for an inconsistency between a belief and a circumstance is solved when the explanation for the inconsistency is credible and valuable (Chapter 2).

12. Credible beliefs are coherent, valid, and true (Chapter 2).

13. Valuable beliefs are significant, comprehensive, and useful (Chapter 2).

14. The more credible and valuable a belief, the more likely that it will be adopted and used to adjust to or to alter a circumstance (Chapter 2).

15. Empirical theorizing solves the problem of not knowing why an explanation for a circumstance is inconsistent with that circumstance (Chapter 3).

16. Moral theorizing solves the problem of not knowing why the moral judgment about the acceptability of a circumstance is inconsistent with the explanation for the cause of that circumstance (Chapter 4).

17. Policy theorizing solves the problem of not knowing why the prescription for action on a circumstance is inconsistent with the explanation for the cause of the circumstance or with a moral judgment about the acceptability of that circumstance (Chapter 5).

18. Constructive theorizing is recursive when the theories it constructs to solve one problem of not understanding create other problems of not understanding that also require constructive theorizing (Chapter 6).

19. Recursive constructive theorizing occurs when the three problems of not knowing are logically related (Chapter 6).

20. The three problems of not knowing are related logically when the empirical problem of not knowing the cause of a circumstance produces a moral problem of not knowing how to judge the circumstance that produces a policy problem of not knowing what to do about the circumstance (Chapter 6).

TABLE 6.5
Theories Constructed and Evaluated With Constructive Theorizing

Chapters	Theories
Chapter 1: Knowing What to Believe	An Empirical Theory About Using Golf Carts A Moral Theory About Using Golf Carts A Policy Theory About Using Golf Carts
Chapter 2: Constructing Credible and Valuable Beliefs	A Theory of Credible and Valuable Beliefs
Chapter 3: Empirical Theorizing About Facts	Autonomy Theory Behavioral Theory Rational Choice Theory Self-Regulation Theory
Chapter 4: Moral Theorizing About Values	Fair Chances Moral Theory
Chapter 5: Policy Theorizing About Actions	Liberal Policy Theory Conservative Policy Theory Welfarist Policy Theory Libertarian Policy Theory Equal Opportunity Theory
Chapter 6: Conclusion and Appendix A	An Empirical Theory About Wheelchair Racing A Moral Theory About Wheelchair Racing A Policy Theory About Wheelchair Racing An Empirical Theory of the Expanding Universe A Moral Theory of the Expanding Universe A Policy Theory of the Expanding Universe An Empirical Theory of Cloning A Moral Theory of Cloning A Policy Theory of Cloning

Table 6.5 lists the 23 theories constructed and evaluated in the book. They include 9 empirical theories, 5 moral theories, and 9 policy theories. Appendix B lists the propositions for each theory.

TABLE 6.6

The Terms and Concepts of Problem Solving, General Theorizing,
and Constructive Theorizing

Problem Solving	General Theorizing	Constructive Theorizing
Action	Adjudication	Coherent theory
Actual state	Deduction	Comprehensive theory
Adjustment	Explanation	Constructive theorizing
Beliefs	Induction	Credible beliefs
Choice	Judgment	Empirical problem
Circumstances	Justification	Empirical theorizing
Evaluation	Legislation	Moral problem
Expectation	Prediction	Moral theorizing
Goal state	Prescription	Policy problem
Means-ends problem solving	Proposition	Policy theorizing
Problem solving	Reason	Recursive theorizing
Result	Reasoning	Significant theory
	Speculation	True theory
	Theorizing	Useful theory
	Theory	Valid theory
		Valuable belief
		Verifiable theory

Table 6.6 lists the terms that describe constructive theorizing, problem solving, practical reasoning, and self-regulated learning. Appendix C provides definitions for them.

A FINAL ARGUMENT FOR THEORIZING

This book demonstrated how to separate the facts, values, and actions of a situation in order to clarify and understand their relationship. It also showed how a thinking strategy assists in learning to theorize better. By discriminating among empirical, moral, and policy questions, you learn to separate questions of fact, value, and action. And by explaining differences and similarities, you discover something you previously did not know about those facts, values, and actions. Finally, by summarizing your explanations in a theory, you reconstruct those facts, values, and actions in a new and a more credible and valuable way.

These are skills that theorizers have used for centuries. The scientist searches for reasons to explain circumstances, the philosopher searches for reasons to judge their moral significance, and the policy maker prescribes adjustments to those circumstances. One sector of the knowledge-producing community focuses on understanding how things work, another on deciding how to judge them, and a third on prescribing what to do about them. And although the content of these lines of inquiry varies, the same thinking applies. Chapters 3 through 5 demonstrated this by using constructive theorizing to cross the boundaries dividing inquiries about what is, what ought to be, and what should be done.

This bridging of boundaries is common practice today. Scientists routinely consider the moral significance of empirical theories as well as their implications for social policy. Philosophers consider the moral significance of the empirical theories developed by scientists as well as the moral implications of various policy theories. And policy theorists employ the empirical and moral theories constructed by scientists and philosophers to support their policy proposals. Professionals of all stripes step outside their disciplines to make claims that they hope are credible and valuable about how things work, how they ought to work, and what ought to be done about them. In other words, new explanations may result from a divided labor, but the use of that knowledge does not remain that way. There are too many demands for answers to difficult questions of our time. This is where the effective theorizer comes into play. That person clarifies problems, issues, and questions by deconstructing the theory-to-practice conundrum in a way that allows for the development of credible and valuable answers.

I hope the theorizing strategy in this book has helped you become one of those masters of explanation.

APPENDIX A

Three Problems and the Sample Theories Generated From Them

PROBLEM 1: ATHLETES WITH DISABILITIES

In a front-page article of the *New York Times* (McKinley, 1999b), Carlos Guzman stated he would never forget last year's New York marathon because he was humiliated by being stopped for nearly half an hour at the Queensboro Bridge to allow lead foot runners to pass ahead of him. Apparently, this incident provoked him and others to file a lawsuit in federal court in Brooklyn alleging that the marathon's organizers discriminated against wheelchair racers and hence violated their protection under the Americans with Disabilities Act. To redress this wrong, wheelchair racers requested a separate wheelchair event in the New York marathon.

This request was unusual because it contradicted my understanding of what disabled athletes have sought in their quest to be fully included in competitive sports. Casey Martin, for example, wanted the PGA to modify its rules to allow him to use a golf cart so that he could compete with nondisabled golfers. The wheelchair racers, in contrast, wanted a separate competition for wheelchairs only. This appears to contradict Casey Martin's request to compete with elite golfers in the same tournament. What I want to know is whether Martin's request to be included in a mainstream tournament is consistent with the requests of other disabled athletes for separate competitions.

Empirical Theorizing: Why Did It Happen?

To answer this question, let us identify the circumstances that provoked the request, whether those circumstances were justified, and what should be done about them. These are the empirical, moral, and policy circumstances surrounding what I did not understand about this unusual event.

Step 1: Define the Discrepancy

The first question is empirical in that it asks what caused wheelchair racers to request a separate event in the first place. Apparently, it was being detained so that foot runners could pass. In a previous New York marathon, Carlos Guzman and other wheelchair racers were stopped for nearly half an hour at the Queensboro Bridge to let lead elite runners pass. Why did this happen? This is the *empirical* problem I want to solve. It can be stated as a discrepancy between knowing that in some marathon races wheelchair contestants have been prevented from racing as fast as they could and not knowing why they were detained. If I know the reasons, then perhaps I can determine whether their detention was justified (moral theorizing) and, if it was not, what should be done about it (policy theorizing).

Step 2: Find Reasons

Further investigation into the facts surrounding the incident yielded the following additional information to explain why (McKinley, 1999b):

- According to wheelchair athletes, over the last two decades wheelchair racing has evolved from an exhibition event aimed mostly at inspiring disabled people to a sport in its own right with specialized equipment.

- Wheelchair racers reach speeds of up to 40 miles an hour going downhill, making it difficult for tired runners to scramble out of the way.

- More than 140 athletes in wheelchairs are expected to compete in the 1999 New York marathon.

- As in most city marathons, the wheelchair athletes start the race half an hour before the first phalanx of elite runners so as to avoid collision between the two groups.

- Trouble arises when the fastest runners, accompanied by cars carrying reporters and race officials, catch up to the slower wheelchair athletes and try to pass them.

- During the 1998 New York marathon, one lane of the Queensboro Bridge was under construction. This left only two lanes for runners, and the police ordered wheelchair competitors to wait until the top runners passed.

- The president of the Road Runners said that "we stopped them for safety reasons, because the lead vehicles were not far behind them and we feared they would be endangered by overcrowding when the lead vehicles reached the bridge" (p. D4)

- Marathon officials also stated that "police and other city officials have decided to hold up the wheelchair athletes for their own safety" (p. D4).

- Some marathon runners have stated that their safety was occasionally at stake too. Though many are sympathetic to the wheelchair athletes, the runners say the wheelchairs can be a hazard.

■ Robert L. Laufer, the Road Runners Club's general counsel says, "New York's marathon presents a unique set of logistical problems because more than 30,000 participants, including more than 140 wheelchair athletes, must cross several bridges and major streets in all five boroughs, but we do try to accommodate them all" (p. D4).

On the basis of these facts, it appears that marathons that accommodate thousands of runners and hundreds of wheelchair racers can create dangerous situations that require intervention by marathon officials. On this basis, I constructed the following theory to explain why wheelchair racers were prevented from completing their race uninterrupted.

An Empirical Theory About Official Intervention in Marathons

1. People with mobility disabilities can compete in and win marathons by using a recently developed wheelchair.

2. When operated by good athletes, these wheelchairs often go much faster than the fastest foot racers can run.

3. This can be dangerous when marathon courses are crowded with thousands of runners and wheelchairs that are moving at high rates of speed.

4. Marathon officials are responsible for guaranteeing the safety of all contestants to the maximum extent possible.

5. Therefore, when crowding between wheelchair racers and runners increases the possibility of collision and injury, officials will request wheelchair racers to slow down so that runners can pass or runners to slow down so that wheelchair racers can pass.

Step 3: Evaluate Credibility and Value

Now let us evaluate the theory. (You can evaluate your theory at the same time.) Does it explain why wheelchair racers were detained in previous marathon races? Do the circumstances described in the *New York Times* article (McKinley, 1999b) conform to the explanation I constructed in this theory? They appear to do so in that the *Times* article described problems encountered when runners and wheelchair racers come into contact. Tired runners scramble out of the way to allow faster moving wheelchair racers to pass, and faster moving wheelchair racers are forced to slow down and allow elite runners to pass.

Is this a credible and valuable account for the interventions taken by marathon officials when wheelchair racers came into contact with runners? Let us find out by considering the theory's credibility first. Is it coherent, valid, and verifiable? The theory is *coherent* to the extent that its propositions contribute to a logical explanation for why wheelchair racers want a separate race. Proposition 1 is similar to the second proposition in the empirical theory developed to explain Casey Martin's request to use a golf cart. It claims that the advent of the racing wheelchair has made marathon races accessible to people with mobility disabilities. Proposition 2 compares the speeds of racing wheelchairs with those of runners. Proposition 3 describes the threat to injury to contestants when runners and wheelchair racers compete in the same marathon. Proposition 4 locates the responsibility for protecting contestants with marathon officials. Proposition 5 concludes that under the conditions described in Propositions 1 through 4, marathon officials are likely to intervene to prevent runners and wheelchair racers from colliding. This intervention may require that wheelchair racers slow down to allow runners to pass or that runners slow down to allow wheelchair racers to pass.

Is this argument *coherent* to you? Are any of its propositions irrelevant to the argument or incompatible with each other? To answer, ask if the reasons in Propositions 1 through 5 explain why wheelchair racers were prevented from completing their race uninterrupted. To test for coherence, eliminate any one of the propositions and then determine if the remaining explanation makes as much sense as the earlier version. If it does, then you have improved coherence. Hence, the earlier version was not as coherent as it could have been. (Hint: eliminate Proposition 1 and see what happens. Does it make a more concise explanation? If it does, then the five-proposition explanation was probably not as coherent as the revised four-proposition explanation.)

Now consider whether the argument is *valid*. Do Propositions 1 through 4 lead to the prediction in Proposition 5 that runners and wheelchair racers are likely to be detained during crowded marathons? Conversely, does the conclusion in Proposition 5 follow from the claims in Propositions 1 through 4? Ask yourself if conclusion in Proposition 5 is true only if those propositions are true. Finally, ask if the theory is *verifiable*. Consider whether there are tests or existing information you can use to support or refute the five propositions. One way to test whether the theory is false is to determine if runners or wheelchair racers have been detained by marathon officials for reasons other than those specified in the propositions.

Now let us examine the theory's worth. Is it a significant, comprehensive, and useful explanation for why wheelchair contestants were detained during previous races? The theory is *significant* if it explains every instance of detainment. Does it do this? It does if every instance was to prevent the risk of injury. There is the possibility that some interventions were caused by other factors, like wanting runners to enter the staging area first. If these reasons are also true, then the theory does not explain all the circumstances of detainment. Hence, it is not as significant as it could be. A theory that also accounted for these slowdowns would be more significant.

To consider the theory's *scope,* ask if it explains a full range of circumstances likely to cause racing officials to intervene during marathon-type races. Can this theory do this? Probably not in its current form because the theory describes only risk factors involving contact between wheelchair racers and runners. Clearly, other accidents in marathon-type races may demand official intervention as well. What happens, for example, when a runner or wheelchair racer collapses and needs medical attention? This warrants intervention to provide needed medical assistance. The theory does not cover these occasions. Therefore, its scope is limited in that respect at least.

Finally, ask if the theory is *useful.* Do its predictions yield secondary benefits for anyone? One possible benefit is to alert officials that having wheelchair racers and runners compete together at the same time increases risk of injury. This in turn may motivate them to avoid trouble by conducting separate races. Another benefit may be that simply having knowledge of possible interventions will tend to motivate runners and wheelchair racers to be careful to avoid contact during the race.

Step 4: Adjust Beliefs

Do you think this theory is credible and valuable enough to adopt? If it is, do you hold other beliefs that are inconsistent with this view? As you consider your answer, remember that acceptance of this theory does not mean you approve of an intervention that slows wheelchair racers and prevents them from completing the course in their best time. It only means you believe the theory offers a good explanation for why contestants may be detained during a race. To consider whether such detention is justified, we must identify their effects on the opportunity of contestants to win.

Moral Theorizing: How Should We Judge It?

Moral theorizing addresses this question, which focuses on determining whether it was right for officials to intervene to prevent wheelchair contestants from completing the marathon in the best time. An answer here may determine whether wheelchair users were treated fairly by marathon officials.

Step 1: Define the Discrepancy

To get a handle on the controversy described in the *New York Times* article (McKinley, 1999b), consider this statement by The Road Runners Club's lawyer:

The Achilles Track Club does its best to accommodate all handicapped people, including wheelchair racers. Organizers have provided special staging areas and recovery areas with accessible toilets. It also gives two honorary awards, but no prize money to disabled racers who perform exceptionally well. (p. D4)

Now consider wheelchair athletes' view of the same event. They claim that wheelchair racing is as legitimate as foot racing and should not be viewed simply as "participating." They expect to *win* and hence object to "being lumped together with blind athletes, amputees, cancer victims, diabetics and people in hand-cranked chairs or electric powered chairs" (McKinley, 1999b, p. D4). They want the same respect that other elite marathon athletes receive.

The discrepancy problem that we want to understand is between the known fact that wheelchair racers have been delayed in previous races and not knowing whether this was justified. Getting to the correct answer is difficult because there are contradictory explanations for the intervention. Marathon officials claim that intervention is necessary to prevent injury, whereas wheelchair racers claim that the intervention is discriminatory and therefore unfair.

Step 2: Find Reasons

To resolve this discrepancy, let us consider the following information, also provided in the *New York Times* article (McKinley, 1999b):

■ Several times over the years, athletes have complained that they were held up during the race so that foot racers could pass them and that in some cases they were prevented from crossing the finish line in Central Park.

■ In 1986, racer Bob Hall complained that a police motorcycle pulled in front of him and slowed his progress to a crawl as he was beginning to pass the lead female racers at the 8-mile mark.

■ Alan Brown, a 32-year-old sports marketing agent from Florida who had trained for 3 years for the marathon, said he was stopped in the 1992 race for 10 minutes by volunteers at the entrance of Central Park to allow the lead foot runner to enter the park alone. Before being halted, Brown had struggled for nearly 10 miles with a broken wrist.

■ Miguel Such, 25, a pro racer from Wilkes-Barre, Pennsylvania, finished first among all participants in last year's marathon at 1 hour, 47 minutes. He says he was not allowed to cross the finish line in the middle, where a ribbon was reserved for foot racers, but was instead shunted off onto a special lane to the right.

■ Daniel L. Brown, attorney for the disabled athletes, claims that race organizers stop wheelchair racers during the race and justify it for safety reasons when, in fact, it is to allow foot runners to go first.

According to these reports, wheelchair racers were delayed for reasons other than safety. Perhaps this is what caused the discrimination complaint in federal court, for if official intervention always resulted in runners' finishing their race in record times but never allowing wheelchair racers to finish theirs in record time, then one group was treated differently than the other group. If this happens, is it right?

The moral theory that I constructed takes two factors into account: the need to intervene to prevent injury and the demand to be fair to all contestants.

A Moral Theory About Official Intervention in Marathons

1. Marathon competitions are fair when they give all athletes the same chance of finishing in their best time.

2. Occasionally marathons that include thousands of competitors create dangerous situations that result in official intervention to prevent injury to contestants.

3. Although official intervention during marathon races may be necessary to prevent injury, it may slow down and prevent some competitors from completing the race in their best time.

4. Official intervention that slows some but not all marathon competitors is unfair to those forced to slow down because it prevents them from having an equal chance of finishing the race in their best time.

5. Therefore, it is unfair for race officials to intervene to prevent any individual or group from completing the race in their best time.

Step 3: Evaluate Credibility and Value

Is this a credible and valuable explanation for judging official intervention during marathon races? The argument is credible to the extent that it is coherent, valid, and verifiable. Consider *coherence* first. Do the propositions offer a coherent argument? To answer, consider each in turn. Proposition 1 defines the fair marathon as one in which every contestant has the same chance of finishing the race in his or her best time. Propositions 2 and 3 identify the unusual circumstance—threat of injury—that compels officials to intervene. Proposition 4 concludes that although these interventions are justified on the safety principle, they are not justified on the fairness principle when they adversely affect some contestants more than others. Proposition 5 concludes that any official intervention that fits the conditions specified in Proposition 4 is unfair.

Is this argument *coherent*? Eliminate any one of the propositions and see if it still makes sense. Alternatively, rearrange the sequence and see if coherence is weakened or strengthened. If any of these experiments recommends a revision, go ahead and revise the explanation and compare it with the original. Then choose the version that is more coherent.

Now consider *validity*. Does Proposition 5 follow from Propositions 1 through 4? Can you eliminate any of those propositions and still infer the conclusion? Or is there a proposition that is missing that will make inferring the conclusion more compelling? Last, assume that one or more of Propositions 1 through 4 are false, and then determine if you can still infer the conclusion to be true. If you can perform any of these operations and answer yes, then the argument is invalid. There is an inconsistency or irrelevancy among the five propositions that needs correcting.

Now ask if the theory is *verifiable*. Can you think of evidence that could be used to support or refute any or all of the propositions? One possibility might be to check the definition in Proposition 1 to see if the circumstance it describes meets the criteria of a fair marathon. Another is to ask marathon officials if protecting contestants from injury is their responsibility. Also, you could ask if it is fair to prevent one group of contestants but not others from completing a race in their best time. Finally, you might ask other members of the marathon racing community whether the reasons specified in the propositions justify official intervention and/or constitute unfair treatment. Do you think information like this would be sufficient to verify or refute the theory?

To evaluate the theory's value, ask if it presents a significant, comprehensive, and useful explanation for why official intervention to protect contestants is judged unfair. The theory is *significant* if it can account for all factors affecting the fairness of official intervention during marathon races. Does it accomplish this? What about interventions for rule violations committed by people using wheelchairs, given that those rules are intended to prevent collision injuries? Are these situations covered by this theory? Does the person committing the violation forego his or her right to continue racing unimpeded? If so, does the theory cover this? It doesn't appear to, at least not in its current form. What would you do to make the theory more significant, if anything?

To evaluate the theory's *scope,* ask if it can be used to judge the fairness of official interventions in other types of marathons—those involving bicycles, cars, or horse-drawn buggies. Obviously, there are safety issues here too. Indeed, in car racing, many collisions occur that adversely affect noncolliding racers. Does this theory clarify the moral status of these official interventions? If so, then the theory's scope is enhanced. If not, is there any modification in the theory that would extend its scope to those situations?

Last, ask yourself if the theory is *useful*. Does holding this belief benefit anyone? To stimulate thinking, consider what would happen if everyone associated with the marathon adopted the theory. Would this settle the debate about official intervention? I think it would help in that it would justify intervention that prevented injury. Adopting the theory would also alert people to the fairness threat imposed by that type of action. And this, in turn, might compel marathon officials to avoid that problem altogether by allowing runners and wheelchair users to compete in separate races. Of course, this is what wheelchair racers wanted. Can you think of other benefits from adopting the theory?

Step 4: Adjust Beliefs

The last step in this episode of moral theorizing is to decide if the theory is credible and valuable enough to adopt. If it is, try to determine the effect of this adoption on other beliefs you hold about marathon racing. Consider this scenario. You have always believed that people run marathon races on foot, not in vehicles. Therefore, it is unfair to allow wheelchair racers to complicate the rules of the race by forcing officials to intervene in ways that only complicate an event that is already difficult to manage. After all, wheelchair racers are latecomers to the marathon tradition. If they want to race, they will have to deal with disruptions they have caused by entering in the first place. Moral reasoning like this will have to be adjusted if not discarded altogether if you adopt my moral theory.

Policy Theorizing:
What Should We Do About It?

For now, let us assume that you have adopted this theory of judgment and are ready to decide what officials ought to do about marathons that include runners and wheelchair racers. This is a question of action rather than a question of fact or value. It is located at that point in the facts-values-actions nexus where the understanding provided by an empirical and a moral theory helps decide what should be done. Again, four-step theorizing will find some answers.

Step 1: Define the Discrepancy

The problem that this phase of theorizing must solve is what to do about runners and wheelchair racers who want to enter prestigious contests like the New York marathon. On the one hand, we know that this combination of contestants is likely to require official interventions to prevent injury that results when runners and racers collide. On the other hand, we know that any intervention of this type may cause some contestants to finish the race at less than their best times and that this may constitute unfair treatment by racing officials. What we do not know is whether there is anything that can or should be done to prevent injury and, at the same time, prevent some individuals or groups from being treated unfairly. In other words, we want to know what marathon officials should do.

Step 2: Find Reasons

To find out what they should do, let us consider some additional information. Let us examine what other marathons facing similar problems have done. The following evidence was also available in the *New York Times* article (McKinley, 1999b):

- Major marathons worldwide, from Berlin to Los Angeles, have separate division races for wheelchairs as well as prize money and awards for winners.

- These wheelchair divisions have become so popular that some elite wheelchair racers, like Franz Nietlishpach of Switzerland, have become widely recognized professionals who tour from event to event, getting endorsements from major corporations as well.

- Marathons in Boston, Chicago, Atlanta, Los Angeles, and Houston have wheelchair divisions with prizes.

- The New York marathon has lagged behind a recent trend in the sport by refusing to create a separate division with prizes for wheelchair racers. It has never had a separate division with prizes for wheelchair athletes.

- According to Robert L. Laufer, attorney for race officials, "I think what they are really looking for ultimately is basically to have a separate wheelchair race with awards and prize money. . . . We haven't gotten to that point yet, but it's something we will consider" (p. D4).

It appears from this that the problem identified in my moral theory has been solved in other marathon races through the addition of a separate division race for wheelchair athletes. This allows runners and wheelchairs to race without the threat of collision. It also provides equivalent prizes, awards, and respect for athletes. On the basis of this information, I constructed the following policy theory to explain what New York marathon officials ought to do and why.

A Policy Theory About Separate Races

1. Marathon competitions are fair when the racing methods used by competitors are comparable in all aspects relevant to producing the fastest time.

2. The racing methods used by the wheelchair racer and the runner are not comparable, and as a consequence elite wheelchair racers can complete races in faster times than can elite runners.

3. This makes competitions between wheelchair racers and runners unfair.

4. Therefore, for marathon competitions to be fair to runners and wheelchair racers alike, they must provide separate races for wheelchair racers and runners.

Step 3: Evaluate Credibility and Value

Do you think this a credible and valuable theory for prescribing how to act on the empirical and moral theories constructed earlier? Let us examine the theory's credibility first by deciding if it is a coherent, valid, and verifiable explanation for what should be done about that empirical and moral reasoning.

This policy explanation appears to be *coherent* in that Propositions 2 through 4 are based on Proposition 1, which defines a fair marathon race. Can you see how they develop from that claim? Is the development in that sequence of reasons logical and understandable? If so, then the argument is coherent. Now consider the *validity* of the conclusion in Proposition 4. Remember, the conclusion is true if all preceding propositions are true and false if any preceding proposition is false. To test for validity, imagine one of the first three propositions to be false, and then ask if it makes sense to claim that the conclusion is true nonetheless. Can you do this? Or does the assumption of a false preceding claim make the argument illogical or meaningless? Next, ask if you can *verify* the theory. Consider each proposition one at a time, and ask if there is evidence that can affirm or disconfirm any of those claims.

Now consider the theory's worth. Is it a significant, comprehensive, and useful method for deciding what should be done about marathon races that include wheelchair racers? To be *significant,* the theory's prescription for action must address all questions of not knowing how to protect wheelchair racers and runners from colliding during races in a way that is fair to all. Does it? It does if every incident of intervention to protect affects all contestants equally. On this score, the theory does well because instituting separate races prevents collisions between runners and wheelchair racers. Hence, any slowdown due to official intervention will affect both groups equally.

Next, examine the theory's *scope.* Does the theory solve other types of problems of unfair treatment? On this question, the theory is rather limited in that it deals only with runners and wheelchair racers. However, you probably could revise the context of Propositions 2 through 4 to fit similar circumstances involving different types of racers who need separate races to guarantee fairness for all. Would this type of revision expand the scope of the theory?

Last, ask yourself if the theory is *useful.* Do people who hold it benefit in some way? Will runners and wheelchair racers benefit by adopting the theory? They will if sharing this belief encourages them to work together to get officials to establish separate races for runners and wheelchair racers. Officials themselves may benefit from holding the theory because then they will avoid being forced to choose between intervening to protect and avoiding intervention to be fair.

Step 4: Adjust Beliefs

To end this demonstration of constructive theorizing, ask if this policy theory is credible and valuable enough to adopt. Consider other beliefs that you or others may hold that may contradict this one. One example is the belief that people in professional sports are the best athletes in the world and that disabled people cannot and should not compete with them under any circumstances. This view would support placing wheelchair racers in a separate but lesser division so they can compete with each other. It would not support establishing a race of equal status to the race for runners. You might have to adjust too many other beliefs about professional sports. How would you deal with a belief like this? Can you envision another round of constructive theorizing that would resolve discrepancies between this position and the one I have developed that assumes that disabled racers deserve equal-status races?

Feel free to pursue this line of theorizing on your own.

PROBLEM 2: THE EXPANDING UNIVERSE

Empirical Theorizing: Why Did It Happen?

To answer the empirical question "Why is the expansion of the universe accelerating?" we first define the discrepancy between what we know and what we don't know about the origin and nature of the universe. Next, we search for reasons that explain what we don't know about the universe that bears on this question of accelerated expansion. Finally, we evaluate the credibility and worth of those reasons and adjust existing beliefs about the universe on the basis of that evaluation.

Step 1: Define the Discrepancy

The discrepancy that provoked cosmologists to theorize anew is between the prediction by the big bang theory that the expansion of the universe will *decelerate* and the observations of astronomers that the expansion is actually *accelerating*. This is indeed provocative because up to now cosmologists believed that the universe was formed by an explosion that propelled matter outward and a subsequent deceleration due to the gravitational pull of matter. Unfortunately, this belief does not explain astronomical observations that the expansion of the universe is still accelerating. The following comparison between the prediction and observations describes the problem in greater detail.

The inflationary big bang theory claims the following to be true:

1. At the beginning of time, all matter in the universe was so densely concentrated that no light was emitted.

2. When this concentrated mass exploded in a big bang, the gravitational force of the exploded matter formed stars and galaxies.

3. Because the force of this explosion was greater than the force of the gravitational pull on exploded parts, the universe expanded.

4. Once the gravitational force of all matter equals the force of the initial explosion, the universe will cease to expand.

5. When gravitational force becomes greater than the force of the explosion, the universe will contract.

6. At some point in time, the universe will cease to expand, either by stabilizing at equilibrium between expansion and contraction or by contracting in a big crunch. Under no circumstances will it expand forever.

7. Therefore, given that the universe is approximately 14 billion years old, the rate of expansion of celestial bodies formed during the first 7 billion years is faster than the rate of expansion of bodies formed during the last 6 billion years. In other words, the expansion of the universe is decelerating.

The following are predictions based on recent observations by astronomers:

1. Galaxies formed in the first half of cosmic time are receding at velocities that are comparable to the velocities of objects from more recent periods.

2. Therefore, the expansion of the universe is accelerating.

3. Moreover, there appears to be insufficient mass in the universe for gravitation to slow this rate of expansion.

4. Therefore, the universe will expand forever (Wilford, 1998b).

Step 2: Find Reasons

To find reasons for this discrepancy, cosmologists are considering the possibility that energy coming from exotic matter counteracts the force of gravity by increasing as matter expands. This causes celestial objects to repel each other, which accelerates the expansion. Cosmologists call this new energy the cosmological constant, a factor Einstein used in his theory of relativity to predict a stable universe. They believe that postulating the presence of this new energy will resolve the discrepancy between theory and observations and, at the same time, support the big bang theory and its prediction that the universe will eventually cease to expand. This revised thinking can be summarized as follows.

An Empirical Theory of the Expanding Universe

1. In the beginning of time, when the concentrated mass of the universe exploded in a big bang, the force of vacuum energy, which increased following the explosion, accelerated the expansion of matter at the same time that a gravitational force acted on matter to form stars and galaxies.

2. Because the explosion of the big bang and the vacuum energy it created are greater than the gravitational force on the exploded matter, the expansion of the universe is likely to accelerate.

3. Therefore, some unknown matter is responsible for the vacuum energy that causes the expansion of the universe to accelerate.

Step 3: Evaluate Credibility and Value

The next step is to decide if this explanation is credible and valuable. Does it resolve the discrepancy in a way that is plausible and worthwhile? To begin, evaluate the theory's credibility by asking if it is coherent, valid, and verifiable.

A theory is *coherent* if its propositions hang together or cohere in a logical way. As you can see, the propositions of this theory cohere in that they describe how three factors—the big bang, gravitation, and vacuum energy—account for the initial explosion, a contraction of matter to form stars and galaxies, and then an accelerated expansion of those new parts to form the recently observed boundaries of the universe. Proposition 1 explains the functions of vacuum energy and gravitation following the explosion, and Proposition 2 explains how these forces interact to cause the universe to expand at an accelerated rate. The propositions cohere in that they do not contradict each other and are all relevant to the explanation.

The theory also appears to be *valid* in that the conclusion in Proposition 3 depends on the truth of Propositions 1 and 2. If either proposition is false, then the conclusion that vacuum energy is present will be false as well; and if the conclusion is false, then either or both of those propositions must be false. On the other hand, if the conclusion in Proposition 3 is true, then Propositions 1 and 2 are likely to be true.

Now decide if the theory is *verifiable*. Here you want to know if there are celestial observations or other evidence that can confirm or refute the theory's propositions. For example, can scientists detect the source of that repulsive energy postulated by the theory? Some believe they can. Astrophysicists speculate that these sources might be X-matter and quintessence, which could also explain the early universe's background cosmic energy (Wilford, 1998c). Discoveries like these might support the theory.

Next consider the theory's worth. Is it significant, comprehensive, and useful? You can judge the theory to be *significant* if it explains more of the variation in rates of movement of celestial bodies than the original theory. For example, can it explain the initial acceleration we are now observing, the ultimate deceleration predicted, and the final stabilization of celestial expansion? Any explanation that covers events ranging from the inception of the universe with the big bang to its stabilization at eternity would probably be significant, given that nothing (in time) would be left unexplained. To evaluate the theory's *scope,* you want to know the extent to which it can explain other events or substances unaccounted for by the big bang theory. For example, if the new theory could predict the existence of some new matter, its scope value would increase proportionately.

Finally, ask if this new explanation is *useful.* Does holding this belief about how the universe works benefit us in some way? If you take the view that no one will be here to experience the fate of the hypothesized accelerating or decelerating universe, the answer is obviously no. However, if you consider the possible secondary benefits of celestial observation and space exploration, you may arrive at a different answer. Remember the movie *Deep Impact*? Space observers detected an unknown object headed for planet earth, and this forewarning allowed us earthlings to minimize its impact. Also, recall that on March 12, 1998, there was a news report that an asteroid was expected to make a pass close to earth in 2028 (Browne, 1998a). It led many of us to believe that knowing about the movement of heavenly bodies is valuable. Perhaps you can think of other benefits from knowing how the universe works. Isn't our space program justified in part by the unexpected benefits of its explorations and discoveries?

Step 4: Adjust Beliefs

The last step in constructive theorizing is to decide if the new theory is credible and valuable enough to adopt. Do you think astronomers, cosmologists, and astrophysicists will adopt it? If so, will they feel the need to adjust other beliefs they hold about the nature of the universe in order to accommodate this new view? Wilford (1998c) considered this in the article "Wary Astronomers Ponder an Accelerating Universe":

> Knowledge of an accelerating expansion could lead to a revised recipe of just what the universe is made of. It could resolve a paradox raised by previous controversial suggestions that the universe appears to be younger than its oldest

stars. It could also *change thinking* about cosmic evolution and the ultimate fate of the universe [italics added]. (p. 2)

Some of this belief adjustment has already occurred with regard to the cosmological constant. Einstein invented the concept to make his theory of relativity predict a stable universe, one that neither expanded nor contracted. Later, he learned that the universe was actually expanding and concluded that the constant was a huge blunder, as George Johnson (1998) described:

> One of the first to get an inkling of what came to be called the Big Bang was Albert Einstein, who absolutely hated the idea. In 1917, he was dismayed to realize that his general theory of relativity implied that the universe was either contracting or expanding. Figuratively slapping his forehead—everybody knew the universe was sitting still—he added a term to equations later called a cosmological constant, a fudge factor intended to cancel out any change in size.
>
> Later, after astronomers had amassed compelling evidence that the galaxies indeed were speeding away from the earth and from each other, Einstein famously called the cosmological constant his "greatest blunder." He may have spoken too soon. Over the years, the constant has been dragged out of the trash can and reconsidered whenever the cosmos wasn't behaving as it should. (p. 3)

Now the constant is being "dragged out of the trash can and reconsidered" to reconcile the big bang theory with recent observations of the universe's dynamic nature.

Moral Theorizing: How Should We Judge It?

This explanation for why the expanding universe is accelerating tells us something about how things work but not about why having this knowledge is important. This creates a problem of not knowing how to judge knowledge like this. Again, constructive theorizing may help develop an informed judgment about the importance of knowing about the expanding universe.

Step 1: Define the Discrepancy

Let us begin by clarifying the problem of not knowing how to judge the importance of knowing why the universe is expanding. Recall that one reason for our confusion about the importance of this knowledge is that we don't know why any of this will matter given that none of us will be around when the predictions of the theory are finally proved or disproved. So let us define this as a discrepancy between knowing that scientists spend a lot of time and money scanning the heavens to determine why the universe is expanding and not knowing why we should care about the knowledge they produce. This is the discrepancy problem provoking us to seek answers.

Step 2: Find Reasons

To commence the search for reasons, consider the argument scientists use to justify basic research of any kind, namely that new discoveries will benefit humankind *eventually*. This is a rationale for many scientific inquiries, and it is the reasoning behind the following moral theory:

A Moral Theory of the Expanding Universe

1. Research on how things work in the natural and social world produces knowledge that may help humankind adjust to changing circumstances.

2. Astronomical study of the universe is a type of research on how things work in the natural world.

3. Inquiry into why the universe is expanding at an accelerated rate is an astronomical study of how the natural world works.

4. Therefore, it is good to know why the universe is expanding at an accelerated rate because this knowledge may one day help humankind adjust to changing circumstances.

Step 3: Evaluate Credibility and Value

Now ask if this explanation for why it is good to know about the expanding universe is credible and valuable. To evaluate credibility, examine the theory's coherence, validity, and verifiability. The theory is *coherent* to the extent that its propositions form logical connections with each other. And the theory is *valid* to the extent that the conclusion follows from its premises. On both criteria, the theory appears to be sound because Proposition 1 implies Proposition 2, which implies Proposition 3, and taken together the three propositions imply the conclusion in Proposition 4.

In consideration of the theory's *verifiability*, ask if there is a test or some existing evidence indicating the truth of its claim that knowing about an accelerating universe is good in some way. Again, we are confronted with the suspicion that no one will care about this knowledge because everyone (including offspring) will be gone long before the fact of an expanding or contracting universe can make a difference in their lives. Hence, they will never know if it is good to have this information rather than some other information. On the other hand, it is always possible some future event will reveal the importance of having this knowledge. Perhaps the best we can conclude is that the theory may be verified in the future.

Next, examine the theory's value. Is it significant, comprehensive, and useful? The theory appears to be most valuable on the scope criterion because it provides a comprehensive explanation for why it is good to know about the underlying nature of human existence: that all matter in the universe will change in predictable directions over the course of eternity. However, on the significance criterion, the theory explains very little that is relevant to life prospects on planet earth now. So from a moral point of view, the theory is comprehensive in that it covers everything but insignificant in that it covers nothing very relevant to life as we know it. Of course, this could change if we faced some extinction-producing event that might be avoided if we were more knowledgeable about the universe. If this happened, we would, of course, evaluate the theory's significance more favorably.

To evaluate the theory's *utility,* ask if there are secondary benefits associated with holding the belief that it is good to understand the expanding universe. Will the research that it stimulates yield anything of use, at least in the coming millennium? Recall that nearly a century ago scientists who believed in relativity—a fairly esoteric theory at the time—commenced work that led to the discovery of atomic energy. Similarly, believers in this theory may discover an energy source that replaces our sun when it burns out. Would this make the theory useful?

Step 4: Adjust Beliefs

Now you can ask if this moral theory is sufficiently credible and valuable for you to adopt. If you think it is, then you must decide if you hold other beliefs about astronomical knowledge that need adjusting. For example, if you hold the belief that knowledge about the universe usually doesn't do anyone any good but that this new belief is different, then you may want to replace that belief with this one. On the other hand, if your existing beliefs are already consistent with this view, you do not need to adjust existing beliefs.

Policy Theorizing:
What Should We Do About It

The last problem that arises is one of not knowing how to act on these theories constructed to explain and judge circumstances associated with the expanding universe. Policy theorizing helps solve this problem.

Step 1: Define the Discrepancy

Begin by focusing on the discrepancy between knowing how things work and how to judge them and not knowing what do about them. According to the empirical theory about the facts, for example, some energy source is responsible for the universe expanding at an accelerated rate. And according to moral theory about those facts, it is a good idea to know why the universe is expanding. This leads to the question of what action should be taken based on these two theories. One possibility is to develop a better knowledge base about the expanding universe, perhaps by resolving *another empirical problem* defined by the discrepancy between the theory that an energy source is responsible for the accelerating universe and the fact that no one knows what it is.

Step 2: Find Reasons

An article entitled "Cosmologists Ponder 'Missing Energy' of the Universe" by John Noble Wilford (1998a) considers the need for this type of action. During a meeting at the Fermi National Laboratory, most scientists agreed

> that [while] the supernova astronomers have made a strong case for an accelerating universe and thus for something like the missing energy . . . no one knows the identity and nature of the missing energy. Scientists with a shrug of shoulders, speak of "something strange" or "funny energy." (p. F1)

> Dr. Christopher T. Hill, a Fermilab particle physicist, complained that so far the hypotheses for vacuum energy "are very ad hoc, not tied into the principle of particle physics." The challenge, he said, is to find an entirely new family of low-mass particles in space. . . .
>
> Neither the cosmological constant nor quintessence appeared to be well enough defined to engender enthusiastic support at the workshop, only questions and suggestions for ways to search for more direct evidence of the vacuum energy. Participants heard proposals for investigating the problem with new X-ray astronomy spacecraft and ground-based and spacecraft surveys in the next decade of cosmic microwave background. (Wilford, 1998a, p. F5)

This discussion suggests that knowing more about the inflationary universe awaits knowledge about the nature and source of this missing energy. The following policy theory prescribes actions in accordance with this thinking or theorizing.

A Policy Theory of the Expanding Universe

1. It is good to have knowledge about how things work in the universe.

2. Current knowledge suggests that the universe is expanding at an accelerated rate because of a new energy source called the cosmological constant.

3. The inflationary big bang theory claims that unknown matter is responsible for this new energy source.

4. Cosmological research to determine the presence of this matter will test this prediction to verify the theory of the expanding universe and at the same time it will improve our knowledge about how the universe works.

5. Therefore, research should be conducted to determine the presence of this unknown matter.

Step 3: Evaluate Credibility and Value

How would you judge the credibility and worth of this theory? First, consider its credibility by asking if the theory offers a coherent, valid, and verifiable account of what should be done about the theories developed to explain and judge the circumstances surrounding the expanding universe. To consider the theory's *coherence,* observe how Proposition 1 restates the conclusion of the moral theory about the good of knowing how the universe works and how Propositions 2 through 4 describe a type of knowledge and knowledge production that promises to produce this type of good. Is this reasoning sufficiently understandable to render the theory coherent?

Now consider the theory's *validity.* Note how Proposition 5 follows from the preceding propositions in that those propositions support the conclusion that cosmological research should be conducted. To demonstrate, answer the question "Why should this research be conducted?" and then use the theory's explanation that (a) producing knowledge about how the universe works is good (Proposition 1) and (b) this research will produce knowledge about how the universe works (Propositions 2-4). Does this conclusion follow logically? It does if you can infer the conclusion from those propositions, which means that if they are true, then the conclusion is likely to be true, and if they are false, the conclusion is also false.

To complete the credibility assessment, think about how the theory might be *verified.* Can scientists test the claim that cosmological research will advance existing knowledge about how the universe works? A recent discovery that neutrino particles have mass suggests such a verification test. According to Browne (1998c), who reported this discovery in the *New York Times,*

Among other things, the finding of neutrino mass might affect theories about the formation and evolution of galaxies and the ultimate fate of the universe. If neutrinos have sufficient mass, their presence throughout the universe would increase the overall mass of the universe, possibly slowing its present expansion. (p. F1)

Next, consider the worth of the policy theory by asking if it provides a significant, comprehensive, and useful prescription for learning more about the expanding universe. The theory is *significant* if the research it prescribes produces knowledge to account for all we want to know about the acceleration of the universe. For example, if it identifies particles responsible for the energy behind the accelerated expansion and if this in turn fully accounts for how the universe behaves, then the theory is significant. On the other hand, if these discoveries account for only part of the observed acceleration, then the theory is not as significant. It did not prescribe actions that yielded a complete understanding of the phenomenon.

We also want to know about the theory's *scope*. Will the research advocated by the theory produce findings that will explain other unexpected events in the universe? If so, the theory is valuable because the actions it prescribed solved other problems of not knowing something. Any time a policy theory covers more ground than defined by its expectations, the actions it prescribes have scope.

Last, ask if the theory is *useful*. Does it provide additional benefits for those who adopt and use it? For example, does the research conducted by those who adopt the theory produce new techniques for cosmological observation? And does the need for these new procedures create manufacturing jobs to build those instruments, for example? If so, then holding this policy theory becomes useful in ways indirectly related to its prescriptions for knowledge-producing action.

Step 4: Adjust Beliefs

The last step of constructive theorizing is to identify existing beliefs that must be adjusted should this new theory be adopted. Suppose, for example, that you decide to adopt the policy theory even though you also believe that cosmological research is usually a waste of time and money. This new adoption would require that you adjust that existing belief. On the other hand, let us suppose that you don't think this theory is very credible or valuable and decide not to adopt it. Then you would feel no need or provocation to make adjustments in your beliefs.

Apparently, some scenario like this may be occurring in Japan, where Japanese and American scientists have discovered that neutrinos have mass, a finding that supports the empirical, moral, and policy theories developed here. Despite this remarkable result, the Japanese government has reduced support for this type of research by 15% this year and may reduce support next year by the same amount. According to the research group's leader, Dr. Yoji Totsuka, "This may mean shutting down the [neutrino] detector for up to six months, which would have devastating effects on our research" (quoted in Browne, 1998b, p. A9). And according to Harvard University physicist Dr. Sheldon L. Glashow, support for this type of research is at risk in many countries: "Sweden is threatening to withdraw from CERN [Europe's high-energy physics consortium] for financial reasons [which] could have a ripple effect reducing the financial commitment of other European nations to the coalition" (quoted in Browne, 1998b, p. A9). Perhaps this is a reminder that new policy theories must be more credible and more valuable than existing policy theories if they are to be adopted and used to support ongoing activities.

Last, consider if adopting this policy theory will affect future research on how the expanding universe works and if this, in turn, will affect the future status of the knowledge base in a way that will provoke new rounds of empirical, moral, and policy theorizing.

PROBLEM 3: CLONING A NEW EWE

Empirical Theorizing: Why Does It Happen?

To answer the empirical question "Why did this cloning procedure work?" begin by defining the problem as a discrepancy between what you know and what you don't know about cloning. Next, find reasons to explain what you don't know. Last, evaluate the credibility and worth of those reasons in order to adjust existing beliefs about cloning as necessary.

Step 1: Define the Discrepancy

The unusual event that provoked this problem of not knowing something was the announcement that an effort to clone an adult sheep had succeeded. This alerted theorizers worldwide to a discrepancy between knowing that past attempts to clone DNA from a strange cell to produce a viable offspring had failed and not knowing why the attempt of Scottish researchers to clone Dolly had succeeded. In the passage below, Gina Kolata (1997d) described this development:

> Although researchers have created genetically identical animals by dividing embryos very early in their development, Dr. Silver [a professor of reproductive biology and animal biotechnology at the University of Wisconsin] said, no one had cloned an animal from an adult until now. Earlier experiments, with frogs, have become a stock story in high school biology, but the experiments never produced cloned adult frogs. The frogs developed only to the tadpole state before dying.

It was even worse with mammals. Researchers could swap DNA from one fertilized egg to another, but they could go no further. "They couldn't even put nuclei from late-state mouse embryos into early mouse embryos," Dr. Silver said. The embryos simply failed to develop and died. (p. 22)

Step 2: Find Reasons

To find out why this cloning attempt worked, consider the explanation for Dolly's existence. Apparently, Wilmut bypassed the standard approach by implanting DNA in a cell during its normal cycle of replication. This allowed the cell to treat the DNA as its own during cell division. The new procedure altered the timing of DNA introduction into the strange cell so that normal cell division could reproduce a clone. The theory explaining how this works is as follows.

An Empirical Theory of Cloning

1. When the DNA from the cell of Animal A is implanted in the cell of Animal B and when that receiving cell subdivides to produce an embryo that grows into an adult Animal C, that animal is a clone of adult Animal A.

2. The implantation of DNA from the cell of one animal to the cell of another will result in cell division and embryonic development when the DNA from the donor cell is in synchrony with the DNA of the recipient cell.

3. Synchrony between the DNA of the donor and recipient cells occurs when the recipient cell is not engaged in cell division during the implantation of the donor DNA.

4. Depriving a cell of nutrients causes the cell to cease cell division, and stimulating that cell with an electric charge causes it to resume cell division.

5. Therefore, depriving a cell of nutrients prior to the implantation of donor DNA and then stimulating that cell with an electric charge following implantation will induce the recipient cell to accept the DNA and then to subdivide to produce an embryo that is a clone of the donor animal.

Step 3: Evaluate Credibility and Value

Now evaluate the credibility and worth of this theory. Consider the theory's credibility by assessing its coherence, validity, and verifiability. By examining the logic of the propositions, you can determine if they *cohere* in an understandable argument. Note that Proposition 1 describes a process that will produce a clone and that Propositions 2 through 4 describe procedures that allow that process to occur. This is coherent in that there are no obvious inconsistencies among the four propositions and none of them are irrelevant to the question of how cloning works. The argument also appears to be *valid* in that the conclusion in Proposition 5 follows logically from the premises in Propositions 1 through 4. This means that if they are true, the conclusion is likely to be true, whereas if any are false, the conclusion is also false.

To consider the theory's *verifiability,* ask if there is any way to know whether the explanation is true. One way is to take the action suggested in Propositions 2 through 4 and compare results with the cloning prediction. This is what Wilmut did when he cloned Dolly. He used the procedure described in Propositions 2 through 4. Your experiment could use the same procedure to test his theory. This is what members of the scientific community want to happen before they accept his explanation.

Now consider the theory's value. Is it a significant, comprehensive, and useful explanation for cloning? To be *significant,* the theory must account for all factors that affect cloning. Does it? Or will other methods work that do not use the procedures described in Propositions 2 through 4? If so, then those methods may suggest an alternative theory for how cloning works. Such an event would compromise the significance of the current theory. This became a possibility with the July 23, 1998, announcement in the *New York Times,* "In Big Advance, Cloning Creates 50 Mice." Did these researchers use a procedure different from that described in our empirical theory, or did they use an approach based on its procedures? The report by Gina Kolata (1998a) suggests the latter:

> In his cloning experiment, begun just a year ago, Dr. Yanagimachi used one of Dr. Wilmut's key ideas, but varied his method.
>
> Dr. Wilmut proposed that the secret to cloning was to put a cell into resting state, so that it was not dividing, before using it to clone. He did this by starving the udder cells so they went into a state of hibernation. Then he slipped one of those cells into a sheep's egg whose own genetic material had been removed and gave the egg a shot of electricity to start the development.
>
> In contrast, Dr. Yanagimachi and Dr. Wakayama started with three types of cells that were already in a resting state: cumulus cells, which cling to eggs like a thick smear of caviar; Sertoti cells, which are the male equivalent of cumulus cells, and brain cells. That experiment indicated that cumulus cells would be easiest to clone, so the scientists homed in on them and used them exclusively.
>
> Dr. Yanagimachi and his colleagues injected the cumulus cell's genetic material into mouse eggs whose own DNA had been removed. They waited six hours to give the egg a chance to reprogram the cumulus cell's DNA and then chemically prodded the egg to start dividing. The process of reprogramming remains a mystery to the scientists. (p. A20)

How does this development affect the significance of Wilmut's theory of cloning?

Now consider the theory's *scope*. Does it explain how cloning works for all living things, plants as well as animals, for example? Or does the theory explain only how cloning works for sheep? Knowing this will determine the theory's scope because the greater the range of cloning outcomes it explains, the more comprehensive the theory is.

Last, consider the theory's *utility*. Does it produce secondary benefits for those who hold it? Wilmut's sponsors believe that it does. They claim that the procedures described by the theory will produce pharmacologically useful proteins for inducing clotting in hemophiliacs. This would benefit hemophiliacs as well as those who produce and market the new drug.

Step 4: Adjust Beliefs

Do you believe that this theory is sufficiently credible and valuable to incorporate into your belief system? If you do, then you may want to adjust other beliefs you hold that are inconsistent with this one. For example, if you are a geneticist and hold the belief that cloning will never work with mammals, then you may want to adjust that belief to conform with this theory. On the other hand, if you already hold the belief that cloning of mammals is possible, then adopting this theory will not contradict your existing views on the matter.

Moral Theorizing:
How Should We Judge It?

Of course, you may also hold beliefs about the practice that have nothing to do with how cloning works. You may believe, for example, that cloning is wrong and should never be done. Moreover, you may not know why you feel that way. So by theorizing constructively, you may be able to explain this belief.

Step 1: Define the Discrepancy

Before passing judgment on the practice, let us consider Kolata's (1997e) description of the moral questions it provokes. She stated that it raises "issues as grand as the possibility of making carbon copies of humans and as mundane, but important, as what will happen to the genetic diversity of livestock if breeders start to clone animals" (p. A1). Kolata (1997e) reported the views of Dr. Kevin FitzGerald, a Jesuit priest and a geneticist at Loyola University, who claims that human cloning will create confusion about the moral status of the human clone:

> Although a clone would be an identical, but much younger, twin of the adult, people are more than just the sum of their genes. A clone of a human being, he

said, would have a different environment than the person whose DNA it carried and so would have to be a different person. It would even have to have a different soul, he added. (p. A1)

FitzGerald concluded that although this new technology may allow us to clone ourselves, "that doesn't mean we'd do it. It would be going against everything we desire for the human race" (quoted in Kolata, 1997e, p. A1). John Robertson, law professor and expert in reproductive rights and bioethics at the University of Texas at Austin, wondered if a cloned person would "have an intellectual property right or basic human right to control their DNA" (quoted in Kolata, 1997e, p. B8). If so, would the act of producing a clone constitute procreation or replication?

These questions illustrate the discrepancy between knowing how to do something and not knowing whether it is right to do it. A similar discrepancy provoked scientists, philosophers, and policy makers to resolve the difference between knowing it was possible to construct an atomic bomb and not knowing if it was the right thing to do. For cloning, the discrepancy is between knowing how to clone humans and not knowing if doing this is right.

Step 2: Find Reasons

In the search for reasons to judge the morality of cloning, consider these reactions to Wilmut's announcement about Dolly. In this country, a member of President Clinton's ethics commission, Professor Alexander Morgan Capron of the University of Southern California, described two arguments for cloning considered by the commission:

> On one side are those who stress "scientific and reproductive freedom." . . . They argue that even though some people are repulsed by the idea of creating genetically identical copies of living people, this country has a strong tradition of not preventing scientific research and not intervening in people's right to reproduce.
> On the other side, Mr. Capron said, are those who emphasize the "sanctity of life and traditional family values." They argue that cloning is fundamentally different from what is normally thought of as reproduction and that it would threaten people's notion of what it means to be human, with a unique identity and with well-defined relationships in a family. (Kolata, 1997b, p. 22)

The argument offered by Wilmut during his press conference on Dolly was that clones could be developed for the purpose of contracting human diseases like cystic fibrosis and then used as test subjects for therapies to counter their effects

(Kolata, 1997d). Lawrence Fisher (1997) reasoned along these lines in the following passage:

> [The] ability to clone adult mammals could encourage the production of transgenic animals with organs suitable for transplants to humans, a possible solution to the chronic shortage of organs. Four small biotechnology companies are racing to develop pigs that may serve as organ donors for humans. Such cross-species operations could be common in a decade, the companies say. (p. B8)

Neal First added that "exciting and astounding benefits are possible in the dairy industry because the cloning of cows could produce superproducers of milk, which would increase production and lower its costs" (quoted in Kolata, 1997d, p. 22).

Clearly, competing values support these different views on the morality of cloning. The moral theory below attempts to reconcile some of them by claiming that cloning is good if it improves life prospects of humans and bad if it places the rights and interests of individual humans at risk.

A Moral Theory of Cloning

1. Cloning to improve the food supply and cloning to provide organs for transplants are examples of how the practice may improve life prospects of humans.

2. Cloning to replicate persons or groups of people destroys the uniqueness of the person who is cloned and the cloned person and, as a consequence, violates their rights as individuals.

3. Therefore, cloning is beneficial if it improves life prospects of individuals and harmful if it destroys individuality or violates human rights.

Step 3: Evaluate Credibility and Value

What do you think about this approach to judging the practice? Is it a credible and valuable theory of judgment? To answer this, consider the six criteria for evaluating the credibility and worth of any theory.

To evaluate the theory's credibility, consider *coherence* first by analyzing the structure of the argument. This reveals that Proposition 1 specifies the conditions under which most people judge cloning to be good whereas Proposition 2 specifies conditions under which most people judge the practice to be bad. Proposition 3, which is derived from those propositions, offers a rule that uses both conditions to judge the practice. Taken together, the three propositions cohere in that the first two are complementary and the third is derived from them. Does this pass the coherence test?

Next, test the theory's *validity* by examining the conclusion in Proposition 3 to see if it follows from the premises in Propositions 1 and 2. If it does, the theory is valid. The conclusion in Proposition 3 is true if Propositions 1 and 2 are true, and false if either is false. Do you think the theory is valid?

Now ask if the theory is *verifiable*. Determine if its premises and conclusion are consistent with the facts—namely that some types of cloning are beneficial for humans and other types are harmful. To test this, consider the outcomes of various cloning practices, perhaps by imagining circumstances in which one type would be beneficial and another would be harmful. Then search for evidence to confirm or refute your claim about the existence of these types. Would this constitute a verification? What else would verify the theory? Do you think there are enough ways to get at its truth to conclude that the theory is verifiable?

Finally, consider the worth of the theory. Is it a valuable explanation for how we should judge cloning? To answer, consider once again the criteria of significance, scope, and utility. This moral theory is *significant* to the extent that the rule it proposes judges the morality of all possible cloning practices. Conversely, it lacks significance to the extent that there are practices it cannot judge adequately.

Can you think of any cloning practices that the theory does not cover that may threaten its significance? One that comes to mind is a practice that improves life prospects of individuals but also threatens their rights. Here, the theory would render a contradictory and perhaps equivocal judgment in that it would judge the practice to be right and wrong. Obviously, this is inadequate because it does not help us judge the practice. If there are other circumstances like this, the theory's significance will suffer. Can you think of any such circumstances?

What about the theory's *scope*? Is it comprehensive enough to resolve a full range of moral issues regarding cloning? Does the theory apply to all human circumstances, for example? It does if terms like *life prospects* and *individual rights* cover all relevant circumstances affecting humans and their relationships with each other. Can you imagine a human condition not included in these conceptual boundaries? You can if you believe that animal cloning will affect the human condition in some way and want it covered by a moral theory of cloning. Given that this practice falls outside the boundaries of the theory, you may judge it to be a limitation in the theory's scope.

Last, ask if the theory is *useful*. Does believing its justification for cloning provide secondary benefits for anyone? One potential benefit is that people sharing this theory will agree on the morality of this controversial practice and, as a consequence, feel a sense of solidarity on the subject, especially if they argued among themselves prior to adopting the theory. This in turn may facilitate cooperation as they decide what to do about it, a point to consider when theorizing about cloning policy. Can you think of other benefits associated with adopting the theory?

Step 4: Adjust Beliefs

Is this moral theory of cloning sufficiently credible and valuable to adopt? If so, do you hold any beliefs that are inconsistent with it? Do you hold the belief, for example, that good usually results from scientific discovery and technological development? If so, then you may have to adjust this belief because adopting this theory claims that some cloning practices are good and some are bad. However, if none of your beliefs is inconsistent with this theory, you can adopt it without the cognitive discomfort of holding incompatible beliefs.

Policy Theorizing: What Should We Do About It?

Now that you have an explanation for the facts and values of cloning, you can determine the actions appropriate given these circumstances. This is the third component of facts-values-action theorizing. Again, four-step theorizing will help you decide what should be done.

Step 1: Define the Discrepancy

One difficulty with deciding what to do is that even though you may agree that some cloning is good and some cloning is bad, you still do not know what should be done in a particular situation. To appreciate this difficulty, consider David A. Bell's (1997) letter to the editor of the *New York Times*:

> It is relatively easy to take a stand against what might be called the vanity cloning of oneself, or the mercenary cloning of great athletes or beauties. But consider the much more difficult case of, say, a 10-year-old girl who has developed a deadly blood disease. Only a bone marrow transplant can save her, but neither her parents nor her siblings are close enough matches.
>
> The parents might try to bear a new child to serve as marrow donor, as an American couple famously did several years ago—but even then, the odds may be against obtaining a match. But a clone of the sick girl would, by definition, offer a 100 percent compatible transplant.
>
> Who is to tell the parents that they cannot take this step to save their daughter's life? And in truth, would it be so terrible for them to take it? (p. A14)

Now consider law professor John Robertson's argument that cloning might be justified for couples with dying babies who want to literally replace their children. Or consider Robertson's argument that it might be okay for infertile couples to want a cloned child who would have their genes (Kolata, 1997b). Do these reasons justify allowing humans to be cloned? Before answering, consider

Gina Maranto's (1997) reaction to these proposals in her letter to the *New York Times* editor:

> The statement by the University of Texas law scholar John Robertson that it might not be reprehensible for a couple to clone a dying child is disquieting.
>
> That Mr. Robertson holds such an opinion is not surprising: he has championed the concept of reproductive freedom and a laissez-faire attitude toward reproductive medicine.
>
> But does anyone honestly believe that replacing a dead child with a genetically identical clone could assuage parents' grief?
>
> The fatuousness of this and other similar "acceptable" uses for cloning merely points out the lengths to which some scientists and science apologists will go to justify what is really just a desire to tinker, to fiddle around and then claim that a technology developed out of that desire satisfied some pressing human or societal need. (p. A14)

These examples illustrate the problem with knowing that cloning can be good or bad depending on the circumstances. You don't know what those circumstances are. Hence, you don't know what should be done in advance of having that information. This is the discrepancy problem we want to solve. It is the difference between knowing that some circumstances justify taking action on cloning practices and not knowing what those circumstances are.

Step 2: Find Reasons

The following information may help solve this problem. It was available shortly after Wilmut's public announcement about Dolly:

- In March 1997, President Clinton imposed a ban on the use of federal money for the cloning of humans. He also requested that researchers voluntarily refrain from using private funds for that purpose. He said that people should "resist the temptation to replicate ourselves" (quoted in Seelye, 1997, p. 13).

- Congress banned the financing of research on human embryos.

- Nevertheless, there are loopholes in Clinton's ban and Congress's prohibition that still permit cloning of humans should the technology be developed.

- At the time of the ban, there was no evidence that any researchers were engaged in human cloning projects.

- A Time/CNN poll found that the public was against cloning: 93% disapproved of the cloning of humans, 66% disapproved of the cloning of animals, and 56% reported that they would not eat meat from cloned animals (Seelye, 1997).

- Dr. Harold Varmus, director of the National Institutes of Health, claimed that given that there was no commercial interest in cloning, the purpose of the ban was to reassure the public and to forestall unneeded legislation.

- Six months after the ban on cloning, attitudes about human cloning changed dramatically in favor of those cloning projects that promised benefits for individuals and for society (Kolata, 1997c).

- Some experts on the law claim that any ban on cloning could not be enforced (Tribe, 1997).

- Within a year after Wilmut's announcement about the cloning of Dolly, physicist Richard Seed of Riverside, Illinois, announced plans to raise money to open a clinic to clone humans (Kolata, 1997c).

- In response, Health and Human Services Secretary Donna E. Shalala stated on the CBS News program *Face the Nation* that Seed "will not do human cloning in this country" ("A Cloning Plan," 1998, p. 15).

These facts can be summarized as follows. First, the public believes the practice is morally questionable. Second, the outright banning of cloning may have a constraining effect on research. Third, there is no practical means of preventing cloning even if the government bans it. And fourth, unacceptable practices like those proposed by Dr. Richard Seed may provoke legislators to ban it anyway. They suggest that governmental regulation to maximize the benefits and minimize the harm of cloning may be justified. The following policy theory uses this reasoning to justify government action.

A Policy Theory of Cloning

1. The purpose of government is to ensure the security and promote the general welfare of all citizens.

2. Discoveries in science often lead to new ways of doing things that promote the general welfare without threatening the security or the rights of individuals.

3. Some discoveries in science lead to new ways of doing things that promote the general welfare but also threaten the security or rights of some individuals.

4. Government should regulate those practices to maximize their benefits and minimize their risks to the public.

5. Cloning is a discovery in science that promotes the general welfare but that also threatens individual rights and well being.

6. Therefore, government should regulate cloning to maximize its gains and minimize its risks.

Step 3: Evaluate Credibility and Value

Does this theory meet the standards of coherence, validity, and verifiability that define a credible theory? And does it meet the standards of significance, scope, and utility that define a valuable theory? Consider the theory's credibility first by asking if it is *coherent.* See if you can follow the reasoning in the propositions. Note that Proposition 1 asserts that the purpose of government is to maintain security and to promote the general welfare, whereas Propositions 2 and 3 claim that although most scientific discoveries are consistent with these goals, some threaten security and the general welfare. Proposition 4 concludes that government should encourage projects that enhance the general welfare (Proposition 2) and prohibit those that place the public at risk (Proposition 3), and Proposition 5 applies this reasoning to the practice of cloning. Finally, Proposition 6 concludes that cloning should be regulated because it fits the criteria specified in Propositions 1 through 5. This reasoning appears to be coherent and valid. Do you agree?

The argument appears to be *valid* in as much as the conclusion in Proposition 6 is based on the claims in Propositions 1 through 5. If they are true, then the conclusion in Proposition 6 is supported. On the other hand, if any of those propositions are false, the conclusion is false. You can check this out by imagining that one or more of these propositions are false and then arguing that the conclusion in Proposition 6 is true. If you can do this and still make sense of the argument, then the theory is invalid because it is illogical to derive a true conclusion from false premises.

To evaluate the theory's *verifiability,* consider how you might test its propositions. To check the truth value of Proposition 1, you could consult the Constitution or federal and state law to see if the purpose of government is, in fact, to maintain security and promote the general welfare. To check the veracity of Propositions 2 and 3, you could identify occasions when scientific discoveries have proved to be both beneficial and threatening to the nation's well-being. And to evaluate the veracity of Proposition 4, you could search for cases in which federal and state law have regulated scientific activity to maximize benefits and minimize risks.

You could also check the veracity of Proposition 5 by considering evidence presented in the debates over cloning. Consider, for example, the claims made in articles by Arthur Caplan (1998) and Gina Kolata (1997a). In "Why the Rush to Ban Cloning," Caplan argued that there are no immediate benefits to cloning humans and that hence "it is clear what the goal of regulation and legislation ought to be: to buy us the time to insure the safety and proper oversight of human cloning" (p. A25). And in "Congress Is Cautioned Against Ban on Human-Cloning Work," Gina Kolata (1997a) reported on testimony before Congress indicating that although cloning poses no immediate threat to the public, it promises immediate benefits:

> There is no immediate crisis, most of the witnesses said, since the methods used in Scotland to clone an adult sheep would need to be made much more efficient before they could be tried on humans.
>
> Cloning research holds glittering promise for medicine, and many scientists fear that a hastily enacted ban might inadvertently halt research that could cure disease and save lives. (p. B11)

How does information like this affect your view of the theory's verifiability?

Now evaluate the theory's worth by asking if it is significant, comprehensive, and useful. To be *significant,* the theory must account for all circumstances of cloning that affect the public interest. This was established in Propositions 1 through 3, which asserted that any scientific development that offered benefits and posed risks should be regulated. Therefore, all cloning activities defined as a scientific development for a benefit at some risk are covered by this policy theory. No cloning activity affecting public safety or welfare is exempt from its prescription for regulation. This is the significance of the theory. It informs us on what to do in all types of cloning circumstances.

Now consider the theory's *scope.* Does its rationale for governmental regulation apply to other scientific and technological developments promising a benefit at some risk? Can you think of any examples for using its argument in those cases? What about the use of atomic energy in power plants? In this case, governmental regulation focused on maximizing the benefit of inexpensive energy while minimizing risks to public safety. Recall, also, what happened when the benefit-to-risk ratio became unacceptable. The plant at Three Mile Island was closed. The Federal Drug Administration routinely engages in this type of oversight in its regulation of prescription drugs by members of the medical profession. When the benefit-to-risk ratio for a drug is unfavorable, the FDA prohibits its production and distribution. Can you think of other cases that could be covered by this type of policy theory? How do these considerations affect your judgment about the theory's scope?

Last, evaluate the theory's *utility* by asking if there are secondary benefits to knowing that the government should regulate cloning. One possibility is political. Recall that 93% of the public disapproves of human cloning and 66% disapproves of animal cloning (Seelye, 1997). Political candidates adopting this theory could benefit by using it to justify regulation of cloning during their campaigns to get votes from people on both sides of the argument. Other people who could benefit from adoption of the policy theory include the attorneys, investigators, consultants, policy analysts, and, of course, federal and state bureaucrats charged with implementing its oversight prescriptions. Can you think of other beneficiaries?

Step 4: Adjust Beliefs

Does this evaluation convince you that the theory is credible and valuable enough to adopt? If it does, you may want to identify other beliefs you hold about governmental regulation that are inconsistent with this theory. For example, if you believe government should never interfere with scientific activity, then adopting this belief will require an adjustment of that belief. On the other hand, if you already believe that governmental regulation is necessary for some types of scientific activity, then no belief adjustments are necessary.

Last, consider if adopting this theory will affect future research on how cloning works and if this, in turn, will affect the future status of its knowledge base in a way that may provoke subsequent rounds of empirical, moral, and policy theorizing.

List of the 23 Empirical, Moral, and Policy Theories

NINE EMPIRICAL THEORIES

1. Empirical Theory About Official Intervention in Marathons

Proposition 1: People with mobility disabilities can compete and win marathons by using a recently developed wheelchair.

Proposition 2: When operated by good athletes, these wheelchairs often go much faster than the fastest foot racers can run.

Proposition 3: This can be dangerous when marathon courses are crowded with thousands of runners and wheelchairs that are moving at high rates of speed.

Proposition 4: Marathon officials are responsible for guaranteeing the safety of all contestants to the maximum extent possible.

Proposition 5: Therefore, when crowding between wheelchair racers and runners increases the possibility of collision and injury, officials will request wheelchair racers to slow down so that runners can pass or runners to slow down so that wheelchair racers can pass.

2. An Empirical Theory of the Expanding Universe

Proposition 1: In the beginning of time, when the concentrated mass of the universe exploded in a big bang, the force of vacuum energy, which increased following the explosion, accelerated the expansion of matter at the same time that a gravitational force acted on matter to form stars and galaxies.

Proposition 2: Because the explosion of the big bang and the vacuum energy it created are greater than the gravitational force on the exploded matter, the expansion of the universe is likely to accelerate.

Proposition 3: Therefore, some unknown matter is responsible for the vacuum energy that causes the expanding universe to accelerate.

3. An Empirical Theory of Cloning

Proposition 1: When the DNA from the cell of Animal A is implanted in the cell of Animal B and when that receiving cell subdivides to produce an embryo that grows into an adult Animal C, that animal is a clone of adult Animal A.

Proposition 2: The implantation of DNA from the cell of one animal to the cell of another will result in cell division and embryonic development when the DNA from the donor cell is in synchrony with the DNA of the recipient cell.

Proposition 3: Synchrony between the DNA of the donor and recipient cells occurs when the recipient cell is not engaged in cell division during the implantation of the donor DNA.

Proposition 4: Depriving a cell of nutrients causes the cell to cease cell division, and stimulating that cell with an electric charge causes it to resume cell division.

Proposition 5: Therefore, depriving a cell of nutrients prior to the implantation of donor DNA and then stimulating that cell with an electric charge following implantation will induce the recipient cell to accept the DNA and then to subdivide to produce an embryo that is a clone of the donor animal.

4. An Empirical Theory About Riding Golf Carts

Proposition 1: Improvements in equipment technology have increased the capacity of many athletes to compete successfully in various sports.

Proposition 2: Some of these technological improvements have made these sporting events accessible to people who otherwise would have been unable to participate.

Proposition 3: The golf cart has made golfing accessible to people with mobility disabilities who otherwise would have been unable to participate due to the long distances between holes.

Proposition 4: Given that use of golf carts is an option for all players at most courses and in many amateur and professional tournaments, there is an increased probability that individuals who cannot walk the course will use a golf cart so that they can compete in these tournaments.

Proposition 5: Therefore, golfers with mobility disabilities who can play competitive golf are likely to request the use of a golf cart so that they can participate in tournament play.

5. Theory of Credible and Valuable Beliefs

Proposition 1: The more credible a belief, the more often it produces expectations that are consistent with circumstances.

Proposition 2: The more valuable a belief, the more often it produces expectations that guide choices and actions.

Proposition 3: The more credible and valuable a belief, the more likely it is that believers will hold that belief because it guides them to set expectations, make choices, and take actions that produce circumstances that are consistent with that belief.

Proposition 4: The greater the knowledge of a believer about credible and valuable beliefs, the more likely it is that the believer will derive expectations, choices, and actions from those beliefs and the more often the circumstances resulting from those actions will be consistent with the beliefs.

Proposition 5: The greater the ability of a believer to evaluate and improve the credibility and value of beliefs, the more often that believer will evaluate and improve beliefs that lack credibility or value.

Proposition 6: Believers who have the knowledge and ability to evaluate and improve beliefs are likely to derive expectations from beliefs that are credible and valuable and, as a consequence, are likely to make choices and take actions to produce circumstances that are consistent with their beliefs.

Prediction 1: Believers who do not get what they need and want because they hold suspect and useless beliefs are likely to want to learn how to improve or replace those beliefs.

Prediction 2: Believers can improve the credibility and value of their beliefs by theorizing constructively to (a) identify discrepancies between beliefs and circumstances, (b) find reasons and construct explanations to eliminate those discrepancies, (c) evaluate the credibility and value of their new beliefs, and (d) adjust other beliefs on the basis of understanding provided by their new beliefs.

Prediction 3: Therefore, believers who do not get what they need and want because they hold suspect and worthless beliefs will strive to improve those beliefs if they have the opportunity to learn the skills of constructive theorizing.

6. Autonomy Theory

Proposition: The value of a person's life is a function of the autonomy that person has in determining the direction and content of his or her pursuits in life.

Prediction: A set of political and social arrangements is good to the extent that it protects and promotes the autonomy of individuals in circumstances where those arrangements apply (Johnston, 1994, p. 70).

7. Behavioral Theory

Proposition: The behavior of all organisms is a function of reinforcement contingencies in the environment.

Prediction: The number of behaviors emitted by an organism will equal the number of reinforcements the organism receives from environmental events.

8. Rational Choice Theory

Proposition: Human choice behavior is a function of the cost/gain ratio of each option.

Prediction: Given information about the costs and gains of different options, individuals will choose the option that produces the greatest gain at the lowest cost.

9. Self-Regulation Theory

Expectation Proposition: The closer to optimal the past gain toward goal attainment (in a previous situation) and the smaller the discrepancy between the actual state and the goal state (in the present situation), the closer to optimal the expectation for gain (to reduce the discrepancy).

Choice Proposition: The closer to optimal the past gain toward goal attainment and the more salient the differences between options, the closer to optimal the choice.

Response Proposition: The closer to optimal the past gain, expectations, and choices, the closer to optimal the distribution of responses between task completion to meet the goal and feedback seeking about goal state-actual state discrepancies, options, task performance, and gain.

Gain Proposition: The closer to optimal the past gain, expectations, choices, and responses, the closer to maximum the gain toward goal attainment.

Prediction: The closer to optimal a person's adjustment to a set of circumstances, the closer to maximum the gain toward goal attainment that the person will experience for that set of circumstances.

FIVE MORAL THEORIES

1. A Moral Theory About Official Intervention in Marathons

Proposition 1: Marathon competitions are fair when they give all athletes the same chance of finishing in their best time.

Proposition 2: Occasionally marathons that include thousands of competitors create dangerous situations that result in official intervention to prevent injury to contestants.

Proposition 3: Although official intervention during marathon races may be necessary to prevent injury, it may slow down and prevent some competitors from completing the race in their best time.

Proposition 4: Official intervention that slows some but not all marathon competitors is unfair to those forced to slow down because it prevents them from having an equal chance of finishing the race in their best time.

Proposition 5: Therefore, it is unfair for race officials to intervene to prevent any individual or group from completing the race in their best time.

2. A Moral Theory of the Expanding Universe

Proposition 1: Research on how things work in the natural and social world produces knowledge that may help humankind adjust to changing circumstances.

Proposition 2: Astronomical study of the universe is a type of research on how things work in the natural world.

Proposition 3: Inquiry into why the universe is expanding at an accelerated rate is an astronomical study of how the natural world works.

Proposition 4: Therefore, it is good to know why the universe is expanding at an accelerated rate because this knowledge may one day help humankind adjust to changing circumstances.

3. A Moral Theory of Cloning

Proposition 1: Cloning to improve the food supply and cloning to provide organs for transplants are examples of how the practice may improve life prospects of humans.

Proposition 2: Cloning to replicate persons or groups of people destroys the uniqueness of the person who is cloned and the cloned person and, as a consequence, violates their rights as individuals.

Proposition 3: Therefore, cloning is beneficial if it improves life prospects of individuals and harmful if it destroys individuality or violates human rights.

4. A Moral Theory About Using Golf Carts

Proposition 1: Open invitations to compete in a sporting event are fair to the extent that all people who want to participate are allowed to compete, regardless of their performance on criteria that are irrelevant to winning the event.

Proposition 2: Using a cart to get from hole to hole is irrelevant to winning in tournament golf.

Proposition 3: Individuals whose physical disabilities prevent them from getting from hole to hole by walking cannot participate in tournament golf without use of a golf cart.

Proposition 4: Therefore, golf tournaments that deny individuals with disabilities the use of a golf cart are unfair because they exclude those persons from tournament play on criteria that are irrelevant to winning the game.

5. Fair Chances Theory

Proposition 1: In all societies, individuals treat others fairly when they are treated fairly.

Proposition 2: In societies guaranteeing freedom for all, prospects for self-determination equalize when individuals respect each other's right to self-determination.

Proposition 3: In a free society, individuals judge distributions of the self-determination experience to be fair when they have the same prospects for self-determination as others in that society.

Proposition 4: Therefore, prospects for freedom are distributed fairly when all members of society have the same chance of engaging in their self-determined pursuits.

NINE POLICY THEORIES

1. A Policy Theory About Separate Races

Proposition 1: Marathon competitions are fair when the racing methods used by competitors are comparable in all aspects relevant to producing the fastest time.

Proposition 2: The racing methods used by the wheelchair racer and the runner are not comparable, and as a consequence elite wheelchair racers can complete races in faster times than can elite runners.

Proposition 3: This makes competitions between wheelchair racers and runners unfair.

Proposition 4: Therefore, for marathon competitions to be fair to runners and wheelchair racers alike, they must provide separate races for wheelchair racers and runners.

2. A Policy Theory of the Expanding Universe

Proposition 1: It is good to have knowledge about how things work in the universe.

Proposition 2: Current knowledge suggests that the universe is expanding at an accelerated rate because of a new energy source called the cosmological constant.

Proposition 3: The inflationary big bang theory claims that unknown matter is responsible for this new energy source.

Proposition 4: Cosmological research to determine the presence of this matter will test this prediction to verify the theory of the expanding universe and at the same time it will improve our knowledge about how the universe works.

Proposition 5: Therefore, research should be conducted to determine the presence of this unknown matter.

3. A Policy Theory of Cloning

Proposition 1: The purpose of government is to ensure the security and to promote the general welfare of all citizens.

Proposition 2: Discoveries in science often lead to new ways of doing things that promote the general welfare without threatening the security or the rights of individuals.

Proposition 3: Some discoveries in science lead to new ways of doing things that promote the general welfare but also threaten the security or rights of some individuals.

Proposition 4: Government should regulate those practices to maximize their benefits and minimize their risks to the public.

Proposition 5: Cloning is a discovery in science that promotes the general welfare but also threatens individual rights and well-being.

Proposition 6: Therefore, government should regulate cloning to maximize its gains and minimize its risks.

4. A Policy Theory About Using Golf Carts

Proposition 1: Discrimination on factors that are irrelevant to one's job responsibilities is unfair.

Proposition 2: The Americans with Disability Act prohibits employment practices that discriminate on disability factors unrelated to one's job responsibilities.

Proposition 3: Tournament golf is a public event that employs individuals who have the skills to compete.

Proposition 4: One of the rules of the Professional Golf Association is that during tournament play all players must walk from hole to hole.

Proposition 5: Some individuals with mobility disabilities have the skills to play tournament golf but need a golf cart to move from hole to hole.

Proposition 6: The PGA rules banning the use of golf carts during tournament play discriminate against these individuals on factors that are irrelevant to playing tournament golf.

Proposition 7: This rule is unfair and in violation of the Americans with Disabilities Act.

Proposition 8: Therefore, the rule must be set aside for people with mobility disabilities.

5. Liberal Policy Theory

Proposition 1: Some individuals experience unfair discrimination due to their status as members of minority groups in society.

Proposition 2: This unfair discrimination creates unfair barriers to their self-determined pursuits.

Proposition 3: These individuals cannot overcome these barriers of unfair discrimination on their own.

Prescription: Given that these individuals are not responsible for these social barriers, they are victims and deserve additional opportunities to overcome their unfortunate circumstances.

6. Conservative Policy Theory

Proposition 1: In a society where every person is free and equal in his or her self-determined pursuits, individuals are responsible for their own actions and the outcomes of those pursuits.

Proposition 2: Some people abuse their freedom by avoiding responsibility and by expecting others to help them when they fail in their pursuits.

Proposition 3: This is unfair to people who take responsibility for their own actions and for the outcomes of their self-determined pursuits.

Prescription: Therefore, all free riders, people who do not take responsibility for their actions and outcomes, should be required to take responsibility for their actions and the outcomes of their self-determined pursuits.

7. Welfarist Policy Theory

Proposition 1: All members of society should be protected equally from unusual circumstances of hardship that are beyond their control.

Proposition 2: Some individuals experience circumstances of hardship because they are helplessly incapable of improving their circumstances.

Proposition 3: These people deserve to be protected from unusual circumstances because these conditions are beyond their control.

Prescription: Therefore, all people in need who are helplessly incapable of controlling their circumstances deserve to be protected from the hardship and misery associated with those circumstances.

8. Libertarian Policy Theory

Proposition 1: In societies that maximize individual liberty by minimizing interference in individual pursuits, all persons have the same opportunity to get what they need and want in life.

Proposition 2: When all persons have the same opportunity to get what they need and want in life, the distribution of those outcomes is fair even though some individuals always tend to be more successful in producing favorable results than others.

Prescription: Because any requirement that people who succeed help those who fail is unfair interference with their freedom of pursuit, the only assistance that can be provided to people who fail is charity.

9. Equal Opportunity Theory

Proposition 1: All individuals have the right to self-determination.

Proposition 2: All societies have some individuals who lack the capacity to self-determine.

Proposition 3: All societies generate unequal opportunities to self-determine.

Proposition 4: Consequently, some individuals do not experience the right to self-determine because they lack the capacity and opportunity to do so.

Prescription: All societies should optimize prospects for self-determination among these least advantaged members by increasing their capacity and improving their opportunity to self-determine.

APPENDIX C

Terms and Definitions
for Constructive Theorizing

Action: behavior resulting from a choice.

Actual state: current circumstances.

Adjudication: the process of deriving or deducing a conclusion about the acceptability of a choice or action from a belief about a set of circumstances.

Adjustment: a change in a belief or a circumstance as a result of an evaluation.

Beliefs: verbal and written predictions, judgments, and prescriptions about material and social circumstances.

Choice: action on one of several options.

Circumstances: a pattern of conditions, factors, or events.

Coherent theory: a rational explanation.

Comprehensive theory: a theory that explains different types of circumstances.

Constructive theorizing: problem solving to (a) describe the discrepancy between understanding and not understanding a set of circumstances, (b) find the reasons that create the discrepancy between understanding and not understanding a set of circumstances, (c) construct a proposition, principle, or law that uses these reasons to explain the circumstances that will reduce the discrepancy, and (d) use a rule to explain the circumstances and adjust other beliefs by returning to the first step (a).

Credible beliefs: predictions, judgments, and prescriptions for circumstances that are coherent, valid, and verified.

165

Deduction: the conceptual process of inferring a conclusion from one or more reasons.

Empirical problem: not knowing the cause of a circumstance.

Empirical theorizing: the process of solving a problem of not knowing the cause of a circumstance.

Evaluation: a comparison of a circumstance with a result expected from an action in order to conclude about the effectiveness of that action.

Expectation: a conclusion about a circumstance based upon a belief about that circumstance.

Explanation: a set of reasons for a circumstance.

Goal state: preferred circumstances.

Induction: the process of finding reasons and constructing explanations for a circumstance.

Judgment: a conclusion induced from information about a circumstance that leads to a conclusion about the acceptability of the circumstance.

Justification: reasons induced from information about a circumstance to conclude about the acceptability of the circumstance.

Legislation: rules induced from information about a circumstance that prescribe or proscribe action on that circumstance.

Means-ends problem solving: a cognitive strategy to (a) find the discrepancy between the goal state and actual state, (b) find an operator that will reduce the discrepancy, (c) apply the operator, and (d) return to the first step (a).

Moral problem: problem of not knowing how to judge a circumstance.

Moral theorizing: the process of solving a problem of not knowing how to judge a circumstance.

Policy problem: the problem of not knowing what action to prescribe for a circumstance.

Policy theorizing: the process of solving a problem of not knowing what action to prescribe for a circumstance.

Prediction: the identification of circumstances that will occur based upon a belief about those circumstances.

Prescription: the process of deriving or deducing expectations, choices, or actions from a judgment about a circumstance.

Problem solving: a strategy to answer the three questions: (a) What is the problem? (b) What are the possible solutions? (c) What is the best solution?

Proposition: a claim that a reason or set of reasons constitutes an explanation for a circumstance or set of circumstances.

Reason: a factor or event identified as a cause or a contributor to the occurrence of another factor or event.

Reasoning: the process of identifying reasons.

Recursive theorizing: the recycling of four-step constructive theorizing to adjust beliefs that are inconsistent with a newly adopted belief.

Result: a change in circumstances produced by an action.

Significant theory: a theory that explains all of the unusual circumstances of the unknown phenomenon.

Speculation: the inductive process of identifying possible reasons for a circumstance.

Theorizing: reasoning to explain a circumstance.

Theory: a sequence of statements explaining the cause of a circumstance, the acceptability of the circumstance, or the actions that should be taken with regard to that circumstance.

True theory: an explanation whose premises and conclusions are consistent with the circumstances.

Useful theory: a theory that can provide guidance for setting expectations, making choices, and taking actions regarding the circumstances it explains.

Valid theory: a theory whose conclusion follows logically from its premises.

Valuable beliefs: claims about material and social circumstances that are significant, comprehensive, and useful.

Verifiable theory: an explanation that can be evaluated to determine its correspondence with circumstances.

APPENDIX C

References

Albelda, R., Folbre, N., & Center for Popular Economics. (1996). *The war on the poor: A defense manual.* New York: New Press.

American Psychological Association. (1993). *Publication manual of the American Psychological Association* (3rd ed.). Washington, DC: Author.

Anderson, D. (1998, January 15). Give Martin a ticket to ride. *New York Times.*

Annett, J. (1969). *Feedback and human behavior.* Baltimore: Penguin.

Ashby, W. R. (1960). *Design for a brain: The origin of adaptive behavior.* New York: John Wiley.

Becker, G. (1986). The economic approach to human behavior. In J. Elster (Ed.), *Rational choice.* New York: New York University Press.

Bell, D. A. (1997, March 2). To the editor. *New York Times.*

Bennett, W. J. (1992). *The de-valuing of America: The fight for our culture and our children.* New York: Summit.

Bergmann, B. R. (1996). *In defense of affirmative action.* New York: Basic Books.

Berkow, I. (1998, February 1). Fairness and riding a golf cart. *New York Times.*

Boaz, D. (1997). *Libertarianism: A primer.* New York: Free Press.

Bobrow, D. B., & Dryzek, J. S. (1987). *Policy analysis by design.* Pittsburgh, PA: University of Pittsburgh Press.

Brown, C. (1998, January 17). Nicklaus says carts shouldn't be allowed. *New York Times.*

Browne, M. W. (1998a, March 12). Asteroid is expected to make a pass close to earth in 2028. *New York Times.*

Browne, M. W. (1998b, June 6). Finances worry neutrino researchers. *New York Times.*

Browne, M. W. (1998c, June 5). Mass found in elusive particle: Universe may never be the same. *New York Times.*

Bullock, C. S., III, Anderson, J. E., & Brady, D. W. (1983). *Public policy in the eighties.* Monterey, CA: Brooks/Cole.

Calvin, W. H. (1990). *The cerebral symphony: Seashore reflections on the structure of consciousness.* New York: Bantam.

Caplan, A. L. (1998, January 28). Why the rush to ban cloning? *New York Times.*

Carville, J. (1996). *We're right, they're wrong: A handbook for spirited progressives.* New York: Random House.

Chambers, M. (1998a, February 12). Judge says disabled golfer may use cart on pro tour. *New York Times.*

Chambers, M.(1998b, February 2). Nike has its money on both sides of disability dispute. *New York Times.*

Chambers, M. (1998c, January 15). Just how level a playing field? *New York Times.*

Chen, H. T. (1990). *Theory-driven evaluations.* Newbury Park, CA: Sage.

A cloning plan leads to vows to outlaw it. (1998, January 12). *New York Times.*

Curtler, H. M. (1993). *Ethical argument: Critical thinking in ethics.* New York: Paragon House.

Davis, P. (1995). *If you came this way: A journey through the lives of the underclass.* New York: John Wiley.

Dewey, J. (1933). *How we think: A restatement of the relation of reflective thinking to the educative process.* Boston: D. C. Heath.

Dewey, J. (1991). *How we think.* Buffalo, NY: Prometheus. (Original work published 1910)

D'Zurilla, T. J., & Golfried, M. R. (1971). Problem solving and behavior modification. *Journal of Abnormal Psychology, 78*(1), 107-126.

Edwards, D. V., & Lippucci, A. (1998). *Practicing American politics: An introduction to government.* New York: Work Publishers.

Fetterman, D. M. (1996). Empowerment evaluation: An introduction to theory and practice. In D. M. Fetterman, S. J. Kaftarian, & A. Wandersman (Eds.), *Empowerment evaluation: Knowledge and tools for self-assessment and accountability* (pp. 3-46). Thousand Oaks, CA: Sage.

Fields, B. (1999, October 24). Casey Martin earns a spot on PGA tour. *New York Times.*

Fisher, A. (1988). *The logic of real arguments.* New York: Cambridge University Press.

Fisher, L. M. (1997, February 24). Cloned animals offer companies faster path to new drugs. *New York Times.*

Flew, A. (1977). *Thinking straight.* Amherst, NY: Prometheus.

Galbraith, J. K. (1996). *The good society: The humane agenda.* Boston: Houghton Mifflin.

Gans, H. J. (1995). *The war against the poor: The underclass and antipoverty policy.* New York: Basic Books.

Gaylin, W., & Jennings, B. (1996). *The perversion of autonomy.* New York: Free Press.

Goodin, R. E. (1985). *Protecting the vulnerable: A reanalysis of our social responsibilities.* Chicago: University of Chicago Press.

Goodin, R. E. (1988). *Reasons for welfare: The political theory of the welfare state.* Princeton, NJ: Princeton University Press.

Gray, T. (1991). *Freedom.* Atlantic Highlands, NY: Humanities Press.

Gruber, H. E. (1974). *Darwin on man: A psychology of scientific creativity.* New York: E. P. Dutton.

Haaga, D. A., & Davison, G. C. (1986). Cognitive change methods. In F. H. Kanfer & A. P. Goldstein (Eds.), *Helping people change* (pp. 236-282). New York: Pergamon.

Harris, C. E., Jr. (1992). *Applying moral theories* (2nd ed.). Belmont, CA: Wadsworth.

Held, D. (1991). Democracy, the nation-state and the global system. In D. Held (Ed.), *Political theory today* (pp. 197-235). Stanford, CA: Stanford University Press.

Hellemans, A., & Bunch, B. (1988). *The timetables of science: A chronology of the most important people and events in the history of science.* New York: Simon & Schuster.

Henry, W. A., III. (1994). *In defense of elitism*. New York: Doubleday.

Herrnstein, R. (1971, September). I.Q. *Atlantic*, pp. 43-64.

Herrnstein, R. J., & Murray, C. (1994). *The bell curve: Intelligence and class structure in American life*. New York: Free Press.

Hogarth, R. M. (1980). *Judgement and choice: The psychology of decision*. New York: John Wiley.

Hogwood, B. W., & Gunn, L. A. (1984). *Policy analysis for the real world*. London: Oxford University Press.

Jackson, H. J., & Boag, P. G. (1981). The efficacy of self-control procedures as motivational strategies with mentally retarded persons: A review of the literature and guidelines for future research. *Australian Journal of Developmental Disabilities, 7*, 65-79.

James, W. (1991). *Pragmatism*. Amherst, NY: Prometheus Books. (Original work published 1907)

Janis, I. L., & Mann, L. (1977). *Decision making: A psychological analysis of conflict, choice, and commitment*. New York: Free Press.

Jeffrey, D. B., & Berger, L. H. (1982). A self-environmental systems model and its implications for behavior change. In K. R. Blankstein & Janet Polivy (Eds.), *Self-control and self-modification of emotional behavior* (pp. 29-69). New York: Plenum.

Johnson, G. (1998, March 8). Once upon a time, there was a big bang theory. *New York Times*.

Johnston, D. (1994). *The idea of a liberal theory: A critique of reconstruction*. Princeton, NJ: Princeton University Press.

Kanfer, F. H., & Hagerman, S. (1981). The role of self-regulation. In L. P. Rehm (Ed.), *Behavior therapy for depression: Present status and future directions* (pp. 143-179). New York: Academic Press.

Katz, M. B. (1986). *In the shadow of the poorhouse: A social history of welfare in America*. New York: Basic Books.

Katz, M. B. (1989). *The undeserving poor: From the war on poverty to the war on welfare*. New York: Pantheon Books.

Kaus, M. (1992). *The end of equality*. New York: Basic Books.

Kelley, D. (1994). *The art of reasoning* (2nd expanded ed.). New York: W. W. Norton.

Kolata, G. (1997a, March 13). Congress is cautioned against ban on human-cloning work. *New York Times*.

Kolata, G. (1997b, June 8). Ethics panel recommends a ban on human cloning. *New York Times*.

Kolata, G. (1997c, December 2). On cloning humans, "never" turns swiftly into "why not." *New York Times*.

Kolata, G. (1997d, February 23). Scientist reports first cloning ever of adult mammal. *New York Times*.

Kolata, G. (1997e, February 23). With cloning of sheep, the ethical ground shifts. *New York Times*.

Kolata, G. (1998a, July 23). In big advance, cloning creates 50 mice. *New York Times*.

Kolata, G. (1998b, January 8). Proposal for human cloning draws dismay and disbelief. *New York Times*.

Levitan, S. A., Gallo, F., & Shapiro, I. (1993). *Working but poor: America's contradiction*. Baltimore: Johns Hopkins University Press.

Lewis, B. A. (1991). *The kid's guide to social action*. Minneapolis: Free Spirit.

Lewis, B. A. (1998). *What do you stand for: A kid's guide to building character*. Minneapolis: Free Spirit.

Lock, L. F., Spirduso, W. W., & Silverman, S. J. (1993). *Proposals that work: A guide for planning dissertations and grant proposals*. Newbury Park, CA: Sage.

Maranto, G. (1997, March 2). To the editor. *New York Times*.

McKinley, J. C., Jr. (1999a, November 8). No stop signs on the course: Also, no prizes at the end of it. *New York Times*.

McKinley, J. C., Jr. (1999b, November 4). Wheelchair racers seek equality with runners. *New York Times*.

Mead, L. M. (1986). *Beyond entitlement: The social obligations of citizenship*. New York: Free Press.

Miller, G. A., Galanter, E., & Pribram, K. H. (1960). *Plans and the structure of behavior*. New York: Holt, Rinehart & Winston.

Missimer, C. A. (1995). *Good arguments: An introduction to critical thinking*. Englewood Cliffs, NJ: Prentice Hall.

Mithaug, D. E. (1993). *Self-regulation theory: How optimal adjustment maximizes gain*. Westport, CT: Praeger.

Mithaug, D. E. (1996). *Equal opportunity theory*. Thousand Oaks, CA: Sage.

Mithaug, D. E., Wehmeyer, M. L., Agran, M., Martin, J. E., & Palmer, S. (1998). The self-determined learning model of instruction. In M. L. Wehmeyer & D. J. Sands (Eds.), *Making it happen: Student involvement in education planning, decision making and instruction* (pp. 299-328). Baltimore: Paul H. Brookes.

Morris, R. (1983). *Dismantling the universe*. New York: Simon & Schuster.

Murray, C. (1984). *Losing ground: American social policy 1950-1980*. New York: Basic Books.

Newell, A., & Simon, H. A. (1972). *Human problem solving*. Englewood Cliffs, NJ: Prentice Hall.

Nobles, C. (1997, January 12). Allowed to use a cart for now, golfer wins Nike tour event. *New York Times*.

Powers, W. T. (1973). *Behavior: The control of perception*. Chicago: Aldine.

Random House. (1995). *Random House Webster's college dictionary*. New York: Author.

Rank, M. R. (1994). *Living on the edge: The realities of welfare in America*. New York: Columbia University Press.

Raspberry, W. (1996, February 23). Why we're losing sight of the common good. *Washington Post*.

Rawls, J. (1971). *A theory of justice*. Cambridge, MA: Harvard University Press.

Raz, J. (1986). *The morality of freedom*. Oxford, UK: Clarendon.

Rorty, R. (1998). Against unity. *Wilson Quarterly, 22*(1), 28-38.

Rose, S. (1982). Group methods. In F. H. Kanfer & A. P. Goldstein (Eds.), *Helping people change* (pp. 437-469). New York: Pergamon.

Sandomir, R. (1998a, February 8). A by-the-book defense versus Martin's reality. *New York Times*.

Sandomir, R. (1998b, February 3). Martin gives the court a look at disfigured leg. *New York Times.*

Sandomir, R.(1998c, February 5). Tearfully, Martin testifies to the growing pain in his leg. *New York Times.*

Sandomir, R. (1998d, February 4). Witness in Martin case disputes fatigue factor. *New York Times.*

Seelye, K. Q. (1997, March 5). Clinton bans federal money for efforts to clone humans. *New York Times.*

Shapiro, J. P. (1993). *No pity: People with disabilities forging a new civil rights movement.* New York: Times Books.

Sidel, R. (1996). *Keeping women and children last: America's war on the poor.* New York: Penguin.

Simon, H. A. (1960). *The new science of management decision.* New York: Harper & Row.

Simon, H. A. (1989). *Models of thought.* New Haven, CT: Yale University Press.

Stone, D. A. (1988). *Policy paradox and political reason.* New York: HarperCollins.

Sulzer-Azaroff, B. (1985). *Achieving educational excellence: Using behavioral strategies.* New York: Holt, Rinehart & Winston.

Taylor, C. (1989). *Sources of the self: The making of the modern identity.* Cambridge, MA: Harvard University Press.

Tribe, L. H. (1997, December 5). Second thoughts on cloning. *New York Times.*

Walton, D. N. (1989). *Informal logic: A handbook for critical argumentation.* New York: Cambridge University Press.

Wattles, J. (1996). *The golden rule.* New York: Oxford University Press.

Weiner, B. (1995). *Judgments of responsibility: A foundation for a theory of social conduct.* New York: Guilford.

Whitman, T., Burgio, L, & Johnston, M. B. (1984). Cognitive behavioral interventions with mentally retarded children. In A. W. Meyers & W. E. Craighead (Eds.), *Cognitive behavior therapy with children.* New York: Plenum.

Wiener, N. (1948). *Cybernetics.* New York: John Wiley.

Wilford, J. N. (1998a, May 5). Cosmologists ponder "missing energy" of the universe. *New York Times.*

Wilford, J. N. (1998b, January 9). New data suggest universe will expand forever. *New York Times.*

Wilford, J. N. (1998c, March 3). Wary astronomers ponder an accelerating universe. *New York Times.*

Wilson, E. O. (1998). Resuming the enlightenment question. *Wilson Quarterly, 22*(1), 16-27.

Wilson, J. (1995). *Thinking with concepts.* New York: Cambridge University Press.

Wiswall, W. (1998, January 29). AP news report [On-line]. Associated Press, America Online.

Wright, J. W. (Ed.). (1990). *The universal almanac, 1990.* New York: Andrews & McMeel.

Zimmerman, B. J., Bonner, S., & Kovach, R. (1996). *Developing self-regulated learners: Beyond achievement to self-efficacy.* Washington, DC: American Psychological Association.

Index

About the Author

ennis E. Mithaug is Professor at Teachers College, Columbia University. He received a BA in psychology from Dartmouth College and an MEd in special education, an MA in sociology, and a PhD in sociology from the University of Washington. He has authored and coauthored many journal articles, chapters, and books, which include *Self-Determined Learning Theory: Predictions, Prescriptions, and Practice* (in press), *Self-Determined Supported Employment* (in press), *Inclusive Schooling: National and International Perspectives* (1998), *Equal Opportunity Theory* (1996), *Self-Regulation Theory: How Optimal Adjustment Maximizes Gain* (1993), *Self-Determined Kids: Raising Satisfied and Successful Children* (1991), *Why Special Education Graduates Fail, How to Teach Them to Succeed* (1988), *When Will Persons in Supported Employment Need Less Support?* (1988), *Prevocational Training for Retarded Students* (1981), *How to Teach Prevocational Skills to Severely Handicapped Persons* (1981), and *Vocational Training for Mentally Retarded Adults* (1980).

Printed in the United States
39111LVS00004B/8